BARRON'S

KEN

One Flew Over the Cuckoo's Nest

BY
Peter Fish

SERIES EDITOR
Michael Spring
Editor, *Literary Cavalcade*
Scholastic Inc.

BARRON'S

BARRON'S EDUCATIONAL SERIES, INC.
Woodbury, New York / London / Toronto / Sydney

ACKNOWLEDGMENTS

We would like to acknowledge the many painstaking hours of work Holly Hughes and Thomas F. Hirsch have devoted to making the *Book Notes* series a success.

All inquiries should be addressed to:
Barron's Educational Series, Inc.
113 Crossways Park Drive
Woodbury, New York 11797

Library of Congress Catalog Card No. 84-18446

International Standard Book No. 0-8120-3433-3

Library of Congress Cataloging in Publication Data
Fish, Peter.
    Ken Kesey's One flew over the cuckoo's nest.

    (Barron's book notes)
    Bibliography: p. 110
    Summary: A guide to reading "One Flew over the Cuckoo's Nest" with a critical and appreciative mind. Includes background on the author's life and times, sample tests, term paper suggestions, and a reading list.
        1. Kesey, Ken. One flew over the cuckoo's nest.
    [1. Kesey, Ken. One flew over the cuckoo's nest.
    2. American literature—History and criticism]
    I. Title. II. Series.
PS3561.E6670533 1984   813'.54   84-18446
ISBN 0-8120-3433-3 (pbk.)

PRINTED IN THE UNITED STATES OF AMERICA

456   550   987654321

CONTENTS

HOW TO USE THIS BOOK

You have to know how to approach literature in order to get the most out of it. This *Barron's Book Notes* volume follows a plan based on methods used by some of the best students to read a work of literature.

Begin with the guide's section on the author's life and times. As you read, try to form a clear picture of the author's personality, circumstances, and motives for writing the work. This background usually will make it easier for you to hear the author's tone of voice, and follow where the author is heading.

Then go over the rest of the introductory material—such sections as those on the plot, characters, setting, themes, and style of the work. Underline, or write down in your notebook, particular things to watch for, such as contrasts between characters and repeated literary devices. At this point, you may want to develop a system of symbols to use in marking your text as you read. (Of course, you should only mark up a book you own, not one that belongs to another person or a school.) Perhaps you will want to use a different letter for each character's name, a different number for each major theme of the book, a different color for each important symbol or literary device. Be prepared to mark up the pages of your book as you read. Put your marks in the margins so you can find them again easily.

Now comes the moment you've been waiting for—the time to start reading the work of literature. You may want to put aside your *Barron's Book Notes* volume until you've read the work all the way through. Or you may want to alternate, reading the *Book Notes* analysis of each section as soon as you have finished reading the corresponding part of the original. Before you move on, reread crucial passages you don't fully understand. (Don't take this guide's analysis for granted—make up your own mind as to what the work means.)

Once you've finished the whole work of literature, you may want to review it right away, so you can firm up your ideas about what it means. You may want to leaf through the book concentrating on passages you marked in reference to one character or one theme. This is also a good time to reread the *Book Notes* introductory material, which pulls together insights on specific topics.

When it comes time to prepare for a test or to write a paper, you'll already have formed ideas about the work. You'll be able to go back through it, refreshing your memory as to the author's exact words and perspective, so that you can support your opinions with evidence drawn straight from the work. Patterns will emerge, and ideas will fall into place; your essay question or term paper will almost write itself. Give yourself a dry run with one of the sample tests in the guide. These tests present both multiple-choice and essay questions. An accompanying section gives answers to the multiple-choice questions as well as suggestions for writing the essays. If you have to select a term paper topic, you may choose one from the list of suggestions in this book. This guide also provides you with a reading list, to help you when you start research for a term paper, and a selection of provocative comments by critics, to spark your thinking before you write.

THE AUTHOR AND HIS TIMES

It is the destiny of some writers to be linked forever with the era that gave them fame. F. Scott Fitzgerald inevitably evokes the 1920s heady mix of jazz and exuberant youth, dinner-jacketed elegance and corrupted dreams. The years just after World War II, when Americans in bustling cities and velvet-lawned suburbs found their new affluence somehow more disturbing than deserved, belong in the same way to John Cheever. So it is with Ken Kesey and the 1960s. Thanks not only to his own writings, but to the writings about him—accounts of chemically heightened days, mystical pronouncements, sudden disappearances and frequent arrests, in newspapers, magazines and especially in Tom Wolfe's book *The Electric Kool-Aid Acid Test*—Kesey has become a symbol of those years when a generation believed they could alter their consciousness and the consciousness of a nation through drugs, sex, and noisy rebellion against society rules. *One Flew Over the Cuckoo's Nest*, Kesey's first novel, published in 1962 when he was only 26, earned unusual critical and popular acclaim. Throughout the decade it was one of the books most likely to be found in college dorm rooms across the country, perhaps lodged on a cinder block and plywood bookshelf between Robert Heinlein's *Stranger in a Strange Land* and Hermann Hesse's *Siddhartha*.

In some ways Kesey may seem an odd candidate for the combination of court jester, pop messiah and serious novelist he eventually became, for on the surface, his boyhood had a Norman Rockwell, straight-arrow wholesomeness to it. Born in La Junta, Colorado, in 1935, Kesey moved when still young with his family to Oregon, the setting for his two novels. His father, a dairyman, taught him the love of the outdoors that is manifest in *Cuckoo's Nest* and in his second book, *Sometimes a Great Notion*. Voted "Most Likely to Succeed" in his class at Springfield High School, Kesey went on to attend the University of Oregon, where he was a star both on the wrestling team and in the Drama Department. Writing, however, was becoming his major interest. His initial efforts were short stories, but after graduation he attempted a novel, which remains unpublished. In 1959, a Woodrow Wilson Fellowship enabled him to enter the creative writing program at Stanford University.

At Stanford, Kesey studied under writers Wallace Stegner, Richard Scowcroft, and Malcolm Cowley, but his life outside the classroom influenced his writing as much as his studies. San Francisco, with its bohemian North Beach district and its reputation as a tolerant nesting-place for beat generation writers like Jack Kerouac, lay only forty miles to the north. Kesey and some kindred spirits formed their own satellite artists' colony adjacent to Stanford, on Perry Lane in Menlo Park. There they wrote, and at the same time experimented with practices—notably drug use— that in a few years' time would, for better or for worse, be disrupting lives across America. Kesey's access to mind-altering substances was made easier when he volunteered for experiments being performed at the Menlo Park Veterans Administration Hospital. There he was given psychedelic drugs, including the little-known LSD, while doctors noted the drugs' effects on him. When the experiments ended, Kesey remained at the hospital, employed now as a psychiatric aide.

Both the drug experiments and the job had an enormous effect on Kesey's writing. He abandoned the novel he had been working on and started a new one, set in a mental hospital—the book that was to become *One Flew Over the Cuckoo's Nest*. His experience as a psychiatric aide gave him insight into the workings of the hospital; many of the Acutes and Chronics described in the novel are thinly-fictionalized versions of patients he saw at the VA, and he even went so far as to arrange a sample electro-shock therapy for himself to see what the treatment was actually like. As for the drug experiments, it was his experience with hallucinogens that let him write so vividly from a schizophrenic's point of view: Chief Bromden's ominous dreams of fog and machinery have their roots in Kesey's own LSD and peyote-induced visions.

Cuckoo's Nest met with critical praise seldom lavished on first novels. "A great new American novelist," said Jack Kerouac, the beat poet whose life and work had profoundly influenced Kesey. The distinguished critic Mark Schorer termed the book "a smashing achievement." And it was a financial success sufficient to allow Kesey two years to research and write his next novel, *Sometimes a Great Notion*. The story of a family of Oregon loggers as fiercely individualistic as Randall McMurphy, it is a more ambitious novel than Kesey's first but perhaps less successful. It was made into a motion picture in 1971. After *Notion's* publication in 1964, Kesey embarked on what was to be an extremely extended vacation, functioning less as a writer than as one of the public entertainers who helped to usher in the Aquarian Age. As recounted in Wolfe's *Electric Kool-Aid Acid Test*, Kesey and his band of "Merry Pranksters" travelled the nation in a psychedelically painted bus, ingested large quantities of drugs, and in general made themselves an almost irresistible target to those groups, like the police, unwilling to tolerate such rambunctious attacks on social conventions. Kesey was arrested three times for possession of marijuana, fled to Mexico after faking a suicide note, and, on his return to California, served five months in jail.

Upon his release, he returned to Oregon to farm and to write, and there, except for sojourns to England and Egypt, he has remained. In 1973, he published a group of short pieces, *Kesey's Garage Sale*. Subsequently he worked on a new novel, portions of which appeared in the magazine *Esquire*.

One Flew Over the Cuckoo's Nest remained widely read and studied well after its publication. A play based on the novel enjoyed long runs off-Broadway and in many parts of the country; the movie made from it (over Kesey's protests) in 1975 garnered all five major Academy Awards, the first film to achieve that feat in nearly 40 years. Clearly, something about the tale of McMurphy and Nurse Ratched fighting for the souls of the Chief and the other patients generates a powerful appeal. Perhaps some of that appeal lies in the book's fast-paced, comic-strip humor, and in the comic-strip simplicity of its distinctions between good and evil. More seriously, the book's message—that one must never be afraid to laugh, nor to rebel against a society that values efficiency and conformity above people—has not staled: it may be more to the point now than it was in 1962. And, despite McMurphy's defeat, this message, too, is a curiously satisfying, optimistic and American one, for it suggests that though the battle will be difficult and will claim some victims, there is a chance it can be won. We see that in Chief Bromden's leap from the ward window out into a world where men can be free.

THE NOVEL

The Plot

A half-Indian named Chief Bromden begins telling us of his experiences in an Oregon mental hospital. His disturbed mind teems with machine-obsessed hallucinations, yet these hallucinations reveal a deeper truth: far from being a place of healing, the hospital is a place of fear. Head of his ward is Nurse Ratched, a woman of great self-control, who, in the Chief's view, is the most powerful of the hospital's mechanical instruments. Only her large breasts betray the fact that she is a human being, and these she has hidden beneath her uniform. The Chief has convinced everyone that he is deaf and dumb; he tries to flee reality by thinking back to his happy childhood in an Indian village. But his dread of a sinister force called the Combine shatters his memories, and in moments of greatest stress a thick fog entirely clouds his mind.

A new patient is admitted: Randall Patrick McMurphy, a loud, red-headed braggart claiming to be in the hospital only to enjoy an easier life than he had at a state work farm. He doesn't seem crazy: with his tales of fighting, gambling, and love-making, he brings laughter into the ward for the first time in years. Immediately he tries to make friends with the other patients, among them shy, stuttering Billy Bibbit, and Dale Harding, an intelligent man ashamed of his effeminacy.

The Nurse and her new patient are in every way opposed to each other, she demanding control, he reveling in freedom. Inevitably, as the Nurse asserts

her power, McMurphy rebels against it, not yet realizing rebellion may be dangerous. Nurse Ratched has
defeated past troublemakers with electro-shock therapy, or with lobotomies—the latter an operation that
makes patients docile members of society at the
expense of their individuality.

At the daily Group Meeting, McMurphy is appalled
at the way Nurse Ratched destroys her patients' self-
confidence, in particular their sexual self-confidence—especially devastating because he believes
freely expressed sexuality is a key to a healthy life. He
bets Harding and the others that he can make the
Nurse lose control of the ward without giving her an
excuse to punish him.

McMurphy's often funny skirmishes with the
Nurse and her staff entertain the patients; increasing-
ly, he reminds the Chief of his father, a full-blooded
Indian Chief who also used laughter to fight his enemies. But when McMurphy proposes that the
patients be allowed to watch the World Series on television, only one, Cheswick, sides with him. Disgusted at this timidity, McMurphy demonstrates how he
might escape by tossing a control panel through a
window. He fails, but his nerve inspires the group to
vote with him at the next meeting. Needing one more
vote, he approaches the Chief, who, fearful of the
freedom McMurphy offers, is cowering in a mental
fog so thick it threatens to engulf him forever. McMurphy's force of personality pulls the Chief out of his
illness. While the Nurse still refuses to let them watch
the Series, McMurphy wins a point by making her
lose control of her temper.

Soon, however, McMurphy learns a painful truth:
he will not leave the hospital until Nurse Ratched
agrees to release him. Nervously, he begins to obey

her rules. But by raising hopes he hasn't fulfilled, McMurphy has left the patients worse off than before. Cheswick becomes so depressed he drowns himself. McMurphy's sense of entrapment grows when he learns that, unlike himself, most of the other patients have voluntarily committed themselves to the hospital. Determined to destroy the fear that's been hammered into them—and in him—he smashes the Nurse's Station window, a symbol of Nurse Ratched's control.

Basking in the glory of another victory, McMurphy arranges a fishing trip for the ward. Long suspecting the Chief can talk and hear, McMurphy speaks to him, and the Chief breaks years of silence to answer. He describes the Combine: people like Nurse Ratched, the government, his own mother, who destroy tradition, nature, and freedom in favor of machinelike conformity. As it did to his father, the Combine has made the Chief "small"—for in his mind psychological defeat creates physical diminution. McMurphy strikes a deal: if the Chief promises to grow large enough to lift the control panel McMurphy could not, McMurphy will let him go on the fishing trip for free.

Out on the ocean, far from the influence of Nurse Ratched, the patients prove they are more capable, more sane than they ever suspected. McMurphy arranges a date between Billy Bibbit and a prostitute, Candy Starr. But on the drive home, the Chief notices that the hospital has worn McMurphy down just as the patients he helped are growing stronger.

Nurse Ratched now turns McMurphy's skill as a gambler against him, convincing the ward's patients he came not to help them but to win their money. McMurphy realizes he must act like the hero the patients require: when an aide abuses one of the patients, George Sorenson, in the shower, McMurphy feels forced to go to George's defense. The Chief joins the fight, and he and McMurphy are sent for electroshock treatments.

As McMurphy is strapped to the treatment table, a parallel is drawn between him and Christ: both have sacrificed themselves for others. During the Chief's treatment, he remembers the forces that brought him to the hospital: World War II, his mother's disrespect for his father, the destruction of his Indian village for a government dam. He remembers the childhood rhyme that gives the book its name and that hints at possible freedom. McMurphy has made him strong enough to withstand the shock treatments: the Chief will never again hide in the fog.

On McMurphy's return, the patients plan his escape, but he insists on waiting until Billy Bibbit has his date with Candy. Billy, prevented from growing up by a domineering mother, will become a man by losing his virginity. When Candy and another prostitute, Sandy, arrive, the ward erupts in a wild party.

McMurphy has suffered too much damage during his stay in the hospital, and he's too weary to attempt to escape when the Nurse arrives in the morning. Billy is discovered with Candy, and Nurse Ratched plays on his guilt feelings until he is once again a stuttering, helpless child. Ashamed, Billy commits suicide by slitting his throat.

The Chief realizes that in the last weeks McMurphy's sole reason for living has been the other patients' needs for him. Now McMurphy makes his last stand, attacking Nurse Ratched. After this humiliation, she will never again regain control of the ward: her face has shown too much fear, her ripped uniform

revealed the breasts that prove she isn't an all-powerful machine but a woman.

McMurphy will never know his victory, though.
His example has given the patients enough courage to
brave the outside world, but he returns from a lobotomy a ruined man. The Chief will not let his friend
remain in this pathetic condition, and he smothers
him with a pillow. Then he goes to the control panel,
which, thanks to McMurphy, he is now "big" enough
to lift, hurls it through a window and escapes.

The Characters

McMurphy

"Do I look like a sane man?" That's the question
Randall Patrick McMurphy asks during his first
Group Meeting, and there's no question that for most
readers the answer will be a quick and resounding
"Yes." McMurphy's sanity takes the ward by storm:
none of the patients have met anyone like him, except
perhaps the Chief, who sees in this red-headed Irishman a hint of his Indian father's humor and bravery.
Where the other patients are timid and quiet, McMurphy is cocky and loud; where they are unable to do
more than snicker, his healthy laughter shakes the
walls; where they are sexually repressed, he is a self-
proclaimed (and, by the evidence, genuine) champion
lover. Years of hard living are etched in his face; to the
hallucination-prone Chief, even his hands can trans-
mit power to make the Chief's own hands larger. The
title McMurphy claims, Bull Goose Looney, with its

connotations of strength and freedom, seems perfectly suited for him.

Much of *Cuckoo's Nest* is devoted to showing how McMurphy teaches the rest of the patients to be sane. What does this sanity consist of? Above all, it is the ability to laugh, both at yourself and at a world that is often ludicrous and cruel. Says Chief Bromden, "He knows you have to laugh at the things that hurt you just to keep yourself in balance, just to keep the world from running you plumb crazy." He may brag, but he never takes himself too seriously. When George Sorenson refuses to shake his "dirty" hand, McMurphy doesn't take offense, merely jokes, "Hand, how do you suppose that old fellow knew all the evil you been into?" And he accepts himself. Where Harding is embarrassed by his "feminine" hands, McMurphy is at ease with his gentler side—his fine handwriting, for example.

Another mark of the sane man is sexual health, for both McMurphy and Kesey see power in sexual terms. One of the ways the Nurse and other members of the Combine destroy men is by making them impotent; the Chief's return to sanity is signalled in part by an erection; Billy will defeat his domineering mother (and Nurse Ratched) when he loses his virginity to Candy. Equally important is a disregard of society's rules and conventions—it's no coincidence that the same girl who first taught McMurphy about sex also taught him that rules (in this case the rule that every sexual encounter must be followed or preceded by marriage) need not be obeyed. Whether he is brushing his teeth with soap powder, letting Martini play his own wild style of Monopoly, or watching a non-existent baseball game on a blank television screen, McMurphy never lets rules—or even common sense—stand in the way of good fun.

Cuckoo's Nest is set in Oregon, and it is very much a novel of the American West: the dream of the free and open frontier is contrasted with the drab and regimented world of the hospital. And just as Chief Bromden recalls the Indian past, McMurphy is in many ways a modernized version of a hero of the old West. He's described repeatedly as a movie cowboy, striding towards a showdown, and at the end of the novel, as the Lone Ranger leaving the town he has saved from the bad guys. He may lack a college education, but he has native intelligence: he knows a pecking party when he sees one.

This, then, is the McMurphy who enters the ward at the start of the book. But he is not a static character; he changes considerably during his time at the hospital. The court that sent him to the hospital ruled him a psychopath; while his diagnosis is so obviously harsh even Dr. Spivey doubts it, we may suspect that it contains just a bit of truth. Among the characteristics of a psychopathic personality are extreme self-centeredness and a disregard for moral and social responsibilities. Certainly McMurphy shows some of those characteristics in the early portion of the book. He came to the hospital only to seek an easier life than he had at the work farm, and at first the battles he fights are fought solely in pursuit of that easy life. They may benefit the other patients, but first they benefit him: it's McMurphy who wants to play cards in the tub room, who wants to watch the World Series. Even the Chief suspects that McMurphy has escaped the Combine because he has "no one to care about, which is what made him free enough to be a good con man."

The same strong instinct for self-preservation that makes him break the rules also makes him obey when he discovers Nurse Ratched's power to keep him in the hospital. But then something happens. One of the patients, Cheswick, who has idolized McMurphy, grows despondent when McMurphy surrenders. He kills himself. McMurphy begins to see that, against his will, he has been saddled with the responsibility of being a hero to men who desperately need a hero. The rest of the book shows him slowly but steadily rising to that responsibility, teaching the other patients—through basketball games and fishing trips—not to let their fears paralyze them. Unfortunately, his generosity is still mixed with a desire for personal gain: he lets George Sorenson go on the fishing trip for $5, not for free; he makes the Chief keep his bargain to lift the control panel so McMurphy can win bets; he demands money from Billy for Candy's visit. This residue of greed convinces the patients that McMurphy was never anything more than a con-man. Only the Chief understands the truth: that at great cost to himself, McMurphy has become the hero the patients require. Their need for him is what keeps his worn out body and spirit going; it's what pushes him to fight for George in the shower, suffer shock treatments, refuse escape until Billy has his date with Candy, and, finally, suicidally, attack Nurse Ratched.

Throughout the book, but particularly in the scene where the Chief and McMurphy undergo shock treatment, parallels are drawn between McMurphy and Christ. While for some it may verge on blasphemy to call this gambler and sinner Christlike, it is true that McMurphy has sacrificed himself for others. In the end the Combine scores what seems to be a complete victory over him; a lobotomy has destroyed him even before the Chief puts an end to his life. Only through the Chief and the other patients who, thanks to McMurphy's courageous example, leave the hospital to fight the Combine elsewhere, does McMurphy live on.

Nurse Ratched

A ratchet: a piece of machinery. That's one of the most important clues to the character of the Nurse who bears a similar name. Nurse Ratched (the name also carries unpleasant echoes of rat and wretched) has transformed herself from a human being into a machine that demands complete control and perfect order from everyone. For the book's other major characters, McMurphy and Chief Bromden, we're given detailed accounts of their life before they entered the hospital. For Nurse Ratched we're given only the barest outlines: that she is about 50, unmarried, a former Army nurse. Why so little? Because the hospital *is* her life: she has shaped it in her image, it has shaped her in its image.

So powerful are the Chief's descriptions of the Nurse as a mechanism of terror, able to swell to tractor size and control the hospital with beams of hate, that it's easy to see the Nurse as the embodiment of pure evil. And because the world of the *Cuckoo's Nest* is in many ways a cartoon world, with good and evil clearly defined, that view is in large part correct. Still, *Cuckoo's Nest* would not be so effective a criticism of the modern world if its characters didn't bear some resemblances to the people we see around us every day. The Nurse is not insane: she could not have risen to her position of power if she were. Nor is she unique in her drive for complete control—she represents forces that influence all of us.

If we were to visit the ward on one of the public relations man's tours, we would probably see the Nurse simply as the strict middle-aged lady Harding describes, the lady the PR man calls Mother Ratched.

She smiles, speaks softly to her aides, bids good morning to her patients. She appears to have the best interests of her ward at heart. She is the voice of common sense: after all, her patients are mentally disturbed; they need some control in their lives.

The Nurse's menace comes from the fact that she has convinced herself that if some control is good, complete control is better. In fact, it's essential, and any threats to it must be destroyed. By putting her goal of complete power ahead of everything else, she perverts the good intentions of the hospital, hiring aides who abuse the patients, and doctors too timid to cure anyone, setting patients spying on one another and turning a useful therapeutic technique, the Group Meeting, into an orgy of shameful psychological backbiting. She destroys the patients' confidence in themselves so they will never be strong enough to leave her.

There's no question that the repression of sexuality is an important part of the Nurse's tactics. She has denied her own sexuality by hiding her large breasts beneath a stiff white uniform and McMurphy's points out that no one could become sexually aroused by her. If, as Harding says, the patients are victims of a matriarchy, Nurse Ratched is certainly the head matriarch. But even McMurphy comes to see that the Nurse's sexual repression is only part of a larger problem—desire for complete control over nature and man that the Nurse shares with much of the modern world.

Chief Bromden

Our guide to the world of the Cuckoo's Nest is the towering Chief Bromden, son of a Columbia Indian Chief, Tee Ah Millatoona (The-Pine-That-Stands-Tallest-on-the-Mountain), and a white woman, Mary

Louise Bromden. In many ways *One Flew Over the Cuckoo's Nest* is as much the Chief's story as it is McMurphy's, and he is as much its hero. For all of the battles McMurphy fights in the ward are fought by the Chief as well; of all the patients, the Chief shows the greatest courage in fighting against the longest odds, and it is only because of his final victory that we are able to hear the story of Cuckoo's Nest at all.

The Chief may seem at first an impossible narrator to know. A man who has for years pretended to be a deaf-mute, his mind is a jumble of seemingly random, terrifying sights and sounds: people swell and shrink according to their power over others; like machines, they shoot electric beams at those who stand in their way. In moments of greatest stress, the Chief's mind becomes entirely clouded by a dense fog. Only when he recalls his Indian boyhood are his thoughts at all clear, and even these happy memories tend to be shattered by his fear of the present.

Yet as we come to make sense of the Chief's visions and nightmare, we see they paint a weirdly accurate picture of the hospital and of the illness that sent him there. He has been damaged by an organization he calls the Combine; in fact, the Combine is just his unstable view of forces that affect every one of us. In the modern world, machines destroy nature, efficiency comes before beauty, and robot-like cooperation is more valued than individual freedom. As an Indian, the Chief was particularly vulnerable. His white mother forced her husband and son to take her name; she helped arrange the sale of the Indian village for a government hydroelectric dam. After these childhood defeats, come many others. Though intelligent and schooled, he can only find menial jobs. His experiences in World War II are so frightening they form the basis for his hallucinations of the fog machine that operates on the ward. He sees his father "shrink"—in his mind, the diminishing is a literal, physical one—from a proud Indian Chief to a man stripped of his name, able to live only off charity from the government that ruined his life. By the time we meet him, the Chief, too, is "small," though his height remains six-feet seven inches. To the aides he is a baby, a household object, as evidenced by their nickname for him, Chief Broom.

McMurphy arrives at a crucial point in the Chief's life. The Chief has endured years in the hospital, years of self-imposed silence, years of abuse. He's undergone over 200 shock treatments. Clearly, he is a strong man. But now, we see, his strength is near its end. He tells us, "One of these days I'll quit straining and let myself go completely, lose myself in the fog." McMurphy's arrival at first seems able only to postpone that day slightly. The Chief is entertained and impressed by the new patient, who reminds him of his father, but he's also frightened of him. The freedom that McMurphy offers is as much a threat as it is a blessing—and the Chief reacts to it as he does to all threats, by cowering in the fog. In fact, by the time McMurphy is battling for his right to watch the World Series, the stress within the Chief is so great it seems he will at last lose himself in the fog completely. It's easier to be lost than to be sensitive to all the pain and injury the Combine has caused, pain and injury that neither he nor anyone else can heal.

But the Chief does not lose himself. Instead, he raises his hand to vote with McMurphy. This is a tribute to McMurphy's strength of character, but it is also a tribute to the Chief's. For as the Chief's hand rises, he at first claims McMurphy is pulling it with invisible strings, just as Nurse Ratched might have. Then he corrects himself: "No. That's not the truth. I lifted it myself." The fact is that the Chief possesses his own reserves of courage—it just took McMurphy to remind him that they were there.

Once this breakthrough is made, the Chief slowly but steadily heals. The fog and the hallucinations come less often, and he is able to remember more of his past and to think about it rationally. With McMurphy he gives up the pretense of being deaf and dumb, allowing himself to share his pain with someone. He recognizes that despite life's anguish, he has to laugh—a sure sign of sanity.

Gradually, too, the man who said he could help no one realizes he must help his rescuer. As the Chief is regaining his power to fight back against the Combine, McMurphy is losing his. When, in the shower, McMurphy fights to protect George Sorenson, the Chief joins in, even though he knows it will lead him to another appointment on the electroshock therapy table. The Chief is able to survive even this: there will be no more fog.

At the end of the book, the roles of McMurphy and the Chief are reversed. McMurphy is weary and near defeat; the Chief has gained strength. Just as the Chief can lift the control panel McMurphy couldn't, he will make the escape McMurphy cannot. After the Chief has smothered his friend out of love for him, he tries on his cap—and finds it's too small. The Chief has regained his true size, and he will be able to fight the Combine on another battlefield.

Dale Harding

The best educated of the men on the ward, Dale Harding is president of the Patients' Council when McMurphy is admitted to the hospital. He serves a useful purpose, both for McMurphy and for us: while the Chief with his hallucinations may give us an

unusual insight into the hospital, Harding gives us
the sorts of rational explanations we're used to hear-
ing. It's Harding who tells McMurphy how Nurse
Ratched is able to maintain her power, how electro-
shock therapy works, what a lobotomy does to people. It's Harding who gives the new patients and the
reader the understanding of the matriarchy Nurse
Ratched directs.

Clever and well-read, Harding can talk smoothly
about psychiatric theory and make joking allusions to
the works of William Faulkner. Yet he is proof that
intelligence alone is not a sufficient defense against
oppression. Harding lacks courage, and lacking courage he can only use his intelligence to deny unpleasant truths, to flee from battles. When McMurphy
points out the viciousness of the Nurse and her Group
Meetings, Harding defends them eloquently, snidely
condemning McMurphy for his lack of education,
even though he knows (and later admits) McMurphy
is completely correct. Harding seems to stand on the
sidelines watching each act of rebellion McMurphy
undertakes, hopeful that the new patient will fail. Perhaps his feeble status is indicated most vividly in his
laugh—or rather, in his inability to laugh: the sound
he makes is painful, "like a nail being crossbarred out
of a plank of green pine."

As with so many of the patients, Harding's problem
is in large part sexual: ashamed of his effeminacy
(symbolized by his graceful, uncontrollable hands),
he is terrified of his wife and her accusations of homosexuality and weakness.

Harding's transformation over the course of the
book is almost as striking as the Chief's. Thanks to
McMurphy, he comes to realize that effeminacy is not

his real problem: the real problem is his fear of it. Following McMurphy's example he is able to overcome his fear, to add courage to his intelligence. The healed Harding is in his way nearly as strong a man as the Chief. He sees the necessity of McMurphy's escape and makes plans for it, and when, unhappily, the escape fails and McMurphy is lobotomized, Harding is able to take on McMurphy's role as card sharp, jokester, and constant irritant to Nurse Ratched. He comes to deserve the title that he couldn't win at the book's start, but which McMurphy bestows on him at the end: Bull Goose Looney. And he is able to leave the hospital in the dignified way he wanted to leave it, met by his wife, ready to start a new life on the outside.

Billy Bibbit

Perhaps the saddest of all Nurse Ratched's victims in *One Flew Over the Cuckoo's Nest* is Billy Bibbit, for he comes so close to not being her victim at all. Sensitive, intelligent, he begins the novel seeming to everyone a mere boy, though in fact he's more than 30 years old.

The most obvious symptom of the illness that has placed Billy in the hospital is his stutter, which, like the Chief's fog and Harding's fluttering hands, grows worse when he is under stress. The stutter forced him out of college and lost him the girl he wanted to marry; interestingly, Billy shares this speech defect, along with an innocence of spirit and a final doom, with another famous Billy of American literature, the title character of Melville's *Billy Budd*—the second obvious reference to Melville in the novel. (The first of course is McMurphy's whale-decorated shorts.)

The stutter, however, is a symptom of a more serious disease: Billy's inability to grow from a boy into a man. Manhood is defined in this book largely in sexual terms, and the fact that Billy has not lost his virginity though he is past 30 shows that he hasn't taken command of his life in other ways as well. As he admits, he lacks guts. The reason? He has been dominated by a mother who will not let him grow up (perhaps, it is hinted, because his growing up would be a sign of her own growing old). Definitely a member of Harding's matriarchy, Mrs. Bibbit has pushed Billy into the hospital; her good friend Nurse Ratched does her best to keep him there.

Just as Billy's plight is defined sexually, so is his recovery. At first he is embarrassed by McMurphy's lewd jokes; soon he is flirting with the nurses and making jokes himself. When McMurphy's prostitute friend, Candy Starr, visits the ward, Billy alone knows how to make her feel at ease with the sort of attention she's used to: a wolf whistle. And on the fishing trip it's obvious Billy is more interested in Candy than he is in salmon.

The attempt to achieve a final cure for Billy brings us to the climax of the novel, as McMurphy arranges for him to lose his virginity to Candy. This arrangement ends disastrously. After enjoying a successful night together, Billy and the prostitute are discovered. For a few minutes, McMurphy's cure seems to have worked. Billy grins fearlessly at Nurse Ratched and wishes her a good morning without stuttering. But in seconds her anger reduces him to a weak "gutless" child again, tongue-tied, begging for her mercy, blaming the situation on everyone but himself. He can't stand this retreat back to the boy he was before; he commits suicide, as he had twice before threatened to do. His death sends McMurphy into his final, fatal battle with the Nurse.

Other Elements

SETTING

The hospital, Dr. Spivey says, "is a little world Inside that is a made-to-scale prototype of the big world Outside." The literary term for such a setting is a microcosm (from the Greek for small universe). Most of the action in *Cuckoo's Nest* takes place in a world that is indeed limited and specific—one ward of one mental hospital in Oregon. But Kesey intends that limited world to serve as a representative of a much larger one.

Mental hospitals have a long and not particularly inspiring history in Europe and America. The first, such as Bedlam in London, became symbols of chaos and cruelty. While waves of reform in the 19th and 20th century improved life for patients somewhat (as the public relations man insists) we see that, at least in Nurse Ratched's ward, abuse both physical and psychological is still rampant.

However, as grim as his descriptions of the hospital are, Kesey is not simply writing a book that criticizes mental health facilities. For we realize that the outside world is not much better. There, Indian villages are destroyed to make way for dams; the landscape is overrun with identical houses for identical businessmen and their identical wives and children. And any attempt to live a life in any way different is crushed. The Chief calls this process the workings of the Combine; we may see it simply as the workings of a modern society. By showing us the similarities between the Inside and the Outside, Kesey makes his book strike with considerable force—for we come to see that the victims of the Nurse and the Combine are not only Harding and Billy and the Chief, but perhaps we ourselves as well.

THEMES

Here are the major themes that Kesey treats in *One Flew Over the Cuckoo's Nest*. They're explained in greater detail in the scene-by-scene discussion of the novel.

1. FREEDOM VS. CONTROL

With McMurphy and Nurse Ratched, Kesey presents two ways of living in the world. McMurphy stands for the individual, the frontier hero who goes his own way no matter what the rest of society thinks. Nurse Ratched represents a desire for efficiency, order, control at all costs. While a case can be made for her view—mental patients undoubtedly need some control of their lives—it's clear that Kesey is on McMurphy's side.

2. THE POWER OF LAUGHTER

McMurphy's greatest strength comes from the way he can laugh at the world and at himself. Like Chief Bromden's father, he knows that the best way to defeat your enemies is by laughing at them. And the degree of sanity of nearly all of the characters in the novel is indicated by their ability to laugh. In the opening scenes no one can; later, the Chief's return to

the real world is signalled by his laugh; when, on the
fishing boat, the entire ward breaks into laughter, it's
a powerful sign of the cure that McMurphy has
worked in them.

3. THE IMPORTANCE OF SEXUALITY

Uninhibited sexuality is a big part of McMurphy's—and Kesey's—idea of sanity. Where sane
men and women are unafraid of sex, many of the
patients—notably Harding and Billy—are in the hospital at least in part because their sexuality has been
thwarted. One of Nurse Ratched's greatest crimes is
that she represses and denies the sexuality of her
patients—and even, with her heavy white uniform,
her own sexuality.

4. THE NEED TO FIGHT FEAR

Many of the patients believe that a single outside
enemy—Nurse Ratched, or the Combine, or a society
that disapproves of homosexuality—has brought
them to the hospital. McMurphy comes to understand that the enemy lies not outside the patients, but
within them—in the fear that makes them easy victims of Nurse Ratched and her allies.

5. THE POWER OF THE MATRIARCHY

When Harding announces that he and the other
patients are victims of the matriarchy, he touches on
one of the most controversial themes in the book. The
repressive power the Chief calls the Combine seems
to be represented mostly by women—Nurse Ratched, Vera Harding, Mrs. Bibbit, Mary Louise Bromden—who force men to obey society's rules and deny
men's sexuality. However, McMurphy admits that
not all "ball-cutters" are female, and other women,
notably the black girl in the cotton mill, are shown to

be victims of the Combine in the same way as are men.

6. WHAT IS CRAZY? WHAT IS SANE?

The patients in the ward have been decreed mentally ill by society, and in some cases, by themselves. Certainly many of them show symptoms that cause us to label them crazy. But the diagnosis of McMurphy as psychotic makes us wonder about the validity of such labels, and when, at the staff meeting, Dr. Spivey and the residents display no more courage or rationality than do their patients, our doubts increase. Even Nurse Ratched's devotion to rules above all else can be seen as a kind of illness, one she shares with much of society.

7. SELF-SACRIFICE

McMurphy enters the ward as a man who, despite his friendliness, thinks of no one but himself. The Chief feels that only by not having anyone to care about has McMurphy been able to escape the Combine. The Chief fully agrees with McMurphy's attitude; he, too thinks it's useless to fight for anyone because the Combine will always win. Gradually, however, McMurphy sees that he's become a hero to the other patients and must act like one even at the risk of his own life. Parallels are drawn between him and Christ: both sacrificed themselves for others. Similarly, the Chief sees that he can't stand completely alone, and he fights alongside McMurphy.

STYLE

The literary style of *One Flew Over the Cuckoo's Nest* is perhaps best analyzed within the book itself, when the Chief describes the ward as looking "like a cartoon world where the figures are flat and outlined in black, jerking through some kind of goofy story that might be real funny if it weren't for the cartoon figures being real guys." Many critics have noted *Cuckoo's Nest's* similarities to comic strips; whether you agree with that analogy or not, you'll probably agree that the book's characters are larger than life, boldly rather than subtly drawn. Nurse Ratched and her aides, for example, aren't so much real people as embodiments of pure malice. Like comic strips, *Cuckoo's Nest* is fast-paced and often very funny.

Indeed, though much of what goes on in the book is grim, humor is one of its hallmarks. Some of it, notably McMurphy's bragging, harkens back to Western tall-tales; the Chief's recollection of Santa's disastrous visit to the ward is black humor, darkened by grotesque irony.

Finally, it's interesting to note that before he became a writer, Kesey had gathered considerable college acting experience and had even tried out for parts in Hollywood motion pictures. Some of that theatrical expertise seems to show in his novel. Take a look at one of the group meetings and see how well he orchestrates them, just as a playwright or screenwriter might, letting each character reveal a little of himself in his words while simultaneously building tension. Perhaps this dramatic skill accounts in part for the novel's successful transformation into a play, and a motion picture.

POINT OF VIEW

Kesey's decision to tell the story of the Cuckoo's Nest from Chief Bromden's point of view, and his mastery of that point of view, are often credited for much of the book's success as a literary work. The Chief's seemingly random and irrational hallucinations, confusing at first, gain clarity when we see that in fact they are carefully organized to give us an understanding of the hospital we would never receive from a more traditional narrator. If we compare the characters' surface appearances to the deeper portrayals of them the Chief gives us, we can see his value. Nurse Ratched may appear a smiling, middle-aged woman to the Public Relations man and his tours; the Chief makes us understand immediately that she has something of the monster about her. If we passed McMurphy on the street, we might think he was nothing more than the scarred veteran of too many bar brawls; but through the Chief's eyes, and so through ours, he is a saviour. Even the Chief himself gains stature because we see him in such close detail. To the aides and other patients he is a towering but deaf and dumb and terrified Indian, irreparably damaged; we know that he is a sensitive, intelligent, noble man, a man well worth all of McMurphy's efforts to save him.

FORM AND STRUCTURE

One Flew Over the Cuckoo's Nest is divided into four parts. Though they differ in length, each part consists of scenes that depict rising tension between McMurphy and Nurse Ratched, culminating in a climatic battle: in Part I, with the fight over the baseball World Series; in Part II, with the smashing of the window of the nurse's station; in Part III, with the fishing trip; in Part IV, with the final fight after Billy's death. Notice that the stakes are continually raised, until the battle in Part IV is fought for the highest stakes of all—life or death.

The Story

PART I

Part I of *One Flew Over the Cuckoo's Nest* is divided into 15 scenes.

SCENE 1

The opening scene is constructed to introduce the reader to two major characters, to hint at themes that will be developed later in the book, and to give readers an understanding of how the novel's somewhat unusual narration and point of view work—to let the readers know what they should believe, and what they shouldn't.

The story begins in medias res (Latin for into the middle of things), without introduction, as if some stranger suddenly grabbed us by the collar and began talking. "They're out there," the narrator begins. Who is out there? And who is speaking? We learn that the narrator is talking about the orderlies in a hospital, that his name is Chief Bromden (shortened to Chief Broom by the orderlies, in honor of his assigned task of sweeping), that he is half-Indian, and that he has fooled the patients and staff into thinking he is deaf and dumb. At the end of the first scene, he lets us know the events he's describing have taken place sometime in the past—the book is a flashback to that time.

NOTE: The Narrator's Point of View.   It won't take you long to see that the Chief's description of the morning's activities in the hospital is in many ways unlikely. It's possible that the orderlies do commit sex acts in the hall (later we're given evidence that the Chief's claim is true), and when the Chief describes their eyes as resembling radio tubes and their talk machinelike humming, he could be speaking in a rational if unusual metaphor. But when he tells us that the Big Nurse, angered by her staff's laziness, swells until she bursts her uniform and reaches the size of a tractor, it's clear we can't trust Chief Bromden to give us the truth—in the usual sense, at least. These are hallucinations; soon we realize that the hospital in which the Chief resides is a mental hospital. We see other aspects of his illness in his mention of a sinister Combine that tries to control him with machinery, and, towards the end of the scene, in his reference to the fog that obscures everything around him. Only when he recalls his Indian boyhood do the Chief's thoughts seem completely coherent. But even that refuge doesn't last: he says, "When I try to place my thoughts in the past and hide there, the fear close at hand seeps in through the memory." The pointer dog used for hunting becomes a bluetick hound, lost and baying in the fog.

Why is this book being narrated by someone so unlikely? Over the course of the novel we will watch the Chief's hallucinations come and go; we will watch the fog advance and retreat. Having the story told by the Chief gives us an unusual, insider's view into a troubled mind and into the forces that trouble it. The Chief's illness and the fight to rescue him from it make up a major portion of the book's plot.

Secondly, though the Chief is a fool, he is like the wise fools of Shakespeare: his words may sound crazy, but beneath their craziness very often lies unexpected sense. The Chief himself signals this fact at the end of the scene, when he says of his story, "But it's the truth even if it didn't happen." In these opening pages, the Chief's hallucinations reveal a skewed but strangely accurate understanding of the hospital, its staff, its patients.

The first major character the Chief introduces us to is the nurse on the ward, and we find a clue to her personality in his earliest mention of her: she opens the door easily because she has "been around locks so long." She is a woman who likes control, and to maintain this control she can imprison people for life. Much of the Chief's description—her purse jammed with gears, her anger that enables her to wrap her arms six times around the orderlies—is so distored it becomes, in a literal sense, impossible. Some of it— her doll-like face, for example—is more or less realistic. But all of his words portray a person who, in her desire for perfection and power, is almost a machine. Even her name, Ratched, possesses a mechanical echo in its similarity to the word ratchet, as in a notched ratchet wrench. The one inconsistency in the nurse is her large, womanly bosom, and this she sees as a flaw. (We'll see the repression of sexuality becoming an important theme in the book.)

The nurse, as the Chief describes her, may be a monster. But if we visited her ward, would we see her that way? After all, she speaks nicely enough to her orderlies, sympathizing with them about "mean old Monday morning," and asking them sweetly to get back to work. Who hasn't heard such words from parents, teachers, employers? But thanks to the Chief's description, we wonder if the sweetness isn't just a tactic, and if there isn't a great hunger for authority and a great rage under that smiling, doll-smooth facade.

SCENES 2 AND 3

The next two scenes show us the hospital and its routine, then introduce us to the character who will shatter that routine.

Chief Bromden, who was drugged after refusing his morning shave, awakens. Although in the past such disobedience has earned him time in the "Shock Shop" (we'll learn the meaning of that unpleasant-sounding phrase later), this morning he was only placed in Seclusion. Now he's back in the day room with the other patients, and he shows us the hospital that is his home.

Both in fact and in literature, mental hospitals have been seen as nightmarish places not of healing but of punishment. Perhaps the most infamous was London's Bedlam, the 18th-century institution whose name is now a synonym for chaos and confusion. The ward run by Nurse Ratched is not bedlam. As the public relations man announces on his tours, it is cheery and bright—not at all like the hospitals of the old days. Indeed, the very fact that citizens are concerned enough about the mentally ill to take tours of the facilities shows that conditions have at least superficially improved.

Yet we know from the Chief that conditions have not improved enough. The public relations man's speech is hypocritical. Portions of the hospital, like the Seclusion room, are dirty; the food (the unsalted mush the Chief sometimes gets) can be bad. More importantly, brutality, both physical and psychological, is rampant. In the first scene we saw the orderlies' pleasure in keeping Chief Bromden under their thumbs: "Big enough to eat apples off my head and he mine me like a baby." Now we're given evidence of sexual assaults against the patients.

The orderlies who frighten the Chief are in turn frightened of the Big Nurse, as of course the patients are too. Her weapons are not—yet—physical ones, but words and threats. The ward is divided into two sections: Acutes (patients who in the staff's opinion can be helped by treatment) and Chronics (those deemed incurable). Nurse Ratched plays on the fears of the Acutes by warning them they will become Chronics if they don't obey her rules. She also encourages the Acutes to spy on each other—by turning patient against patient, she prevents them from turning against her.

Into this grim, rigid setting comes the hero of the novel.

NOTE: McMurphy   We saw clues to the Big Nurse's character in the first sentence about her; we now see clues to McMurphy's in the first sentence the Chief uses to describe him. He is "no ordinary admission."

McMurphy is painted in a way that shows how completely different he is from the patients who have entered the hospital before him. His voice is too loud: "He sounds like he's way above them, talking down, like he's sailing fifty yards overhead, hollering at those below on the ground." (That description may bring to mind a bird soaring overhead, and we'll see the image of birds, linked to flight and freedom, repeated throughout the book, even in the rhyme that provides its title.) McMurphy's voice reminds the Chief of his father; and though McMurphy doesn't look like the elder Indian (instead, with his red hair, he resembles the stereotypical hot-blooded Irishman), he is similarly toughened from hard outdoor work. Perhaps most important is McMurphy's laugh. The public relations man has a false, silly laugh; the Acute patients can only snicker in their fists. (Later we'll hear one, Harding, attempt a laugh and make only a sound "like a nail being crossbarred out of a plank of green pine." McMurphy's laugh is the first real laugh the Chief has heard in years, a brave indication of strength and sanity.

McMurphy's name, too, has meaning. Just as Ratched shows the nurse's machinelike personality, and Chief Broom the Indian's diminishment to a mere household object, McMurphy's initials hint at the effect he's about to have on the ward: R.P.M., identical to the acronym for revolutions per minute found on phonograph records. And a revolution is just what McMurphy will bring.

McMurphy, the new patient can't take a step without disrupting normal hospital procedure. He won't shower; he won't stand still to have his temperature taken. He ignores the division between Chronics and Acutes, greeting everyone like a sideshow pitchman.

Is he crazy? It doesn't seem so. He claims to be in the hospital only because a court ruled him psychotic, claims the ruling came only because he'd had too many fights and too many women. He's glad to enter the hospital, he says; he expects an easier life than he found on the state work farm.

The memory of the frontier West is apparent in much of this book, which geographical clues tell us is set in Oregon. And just as the Chief reminds us of the Indian past, McMurphy with his bragging charm may remind us of the rough cowboy of Western novels and movies. His humor is a modernized version of the tall tales told by and about Western legends like Davy Crockett, Mike Finn, and Paul Bunyan. For example, in his mock showdown with Harding, the college-educated man who is president of the Patients' Council, he wins by bragging he's so crazy he voted for President Eisenhower not once but twice and is going to vote for him again. (The book is set just before the 1960 presidential election. Of course, Eisenhower, who won the 1952 and 1956 elections, could not run for a third term.)

Notice, too, the title McMurphy fights Harding for: Bull Goose Looney brings back the image of McMurphy's high-flying voice, and geese as symbols of freedom will recur often. Bull also implies the powerful sexuality that McMurphy possesses.

Initially McMurphy's antics unnerve the patients, but soon their fears give way to the pleasure of seeing someone disrupt the hospital routine. Even the Chronics seem amused, but when McMurphy approaches the Chief, the Indian's mood changes: the laughter that a moment before he enjoyed now seems frightening, a signal that tells McMurphy the Chief is not really deaf and dumb. This is doubtful (though McMurphy will guess the Chief's secret later), but it's a sign of the new patient's strong personality that the Chief believes it to be true.

The Chief shakes McMurphy's hand. All through the book hands will be used to indicate character, and in McMurphy's we see calloused traces of his entire hard-working, hard-fighting life. As for the Chief's hands, he is an enormous man—six-feet seven inches—and undoubtedly they are much larger than McMurphy's. But the Chief's illness has changed his perception of strength and size: to him, psychological weakness creates physical weakness, and he has been so damaged that he thinks of himself as small. However, when the two shake hands, the Chief feels power being transmitted from McMurphy to him, and sees his hand becoming larger—the first example of McMurphy's healing effect on the Chief.

The handshake is interrupted by the Big Nurse, who warns McMurphy that he must follow the same rules as everyone else.

NOTE: Foreshadowing   One of the literary techniques employed most successfully in the early pages of the novel is foreshadowing, or the use of small events to hint at more important events that occur later. The scene in which McMurphy enters the hospital is largely comic, but it contains examples of foreshadowing that give us indications of less comic events to come.

The first example is Billy Bibbit's comment, "If I was d-d-deaf, I would kill myself." Seemingly casual, Billy's thought of suicide will be repeated later—and, at the book's climax, acted on.

More elaborate foreshadowing can be seen in the characters of Ellis and Ruckley. Ellis is a victim of the already-mentioned Shock Shop—of electro-shock therapy, a treatment once used on certain types of mental patients, in which electricity is passed through the brain. Normally the treatments are short, and their effect, while disorienting, temporary. But in Ellis' case a mistake was made and permanent damage was done. Now he stands spread-armed against the wall, as if his hands had been nailed to the plaster. (The posture is purposely reminiscent of the crucified Christ: the connection between the Shock Shop and the crucifixion—and McMurphy as Christ—will be made more explicit later in the book.)

Ruckley is a victim of another once common treatment, the prefontal lobotomy, in which a portion of the patient's brain is removed. Ruckley, operated on when the technique was still new, has been left unable to do anything but stare at a blank photograph. Now, the Chief says, the operation has been refined; patients are able to go home and lead normal lives of a sort. But the Chief wonders if this fate is any better than Ruckley's. This question, too, will reappear at the book's climax.

Ellis and Ruckley let us know that, while much of what happens in the hospital is wildly funny, human lives are at stake. At the end of the third scene, McMurphy has his first encounter with Nurse Ratched. Everyone must obey, she warns; McMurphy warns that he will do the opposite. The earlier showdown between McMurphy and Harding was a joke. This showdown is real. And while the battles between McMurphy and Nurse Ratched may seem trivial, fought as they are over toothpaste, the World Series, and fishing trips, the presence of Ellis and Ruckley are grim reminders that the war is deadly serious indeed.

SCENE 4

Scene 4 proves that Chief Bromden's trick of seeming to be deaf and dumb is a highly useful one—he can loiter, broom in hand, to catch conversations off-limits to patients. Nurse Ratched is discussing McMurphy with a silly junior nurse. She warns that the new patient is a manipulator, a psychologist's term for someone who thinks of nothing but his own gain. Because McMurphy has told us a bit of his history as gambler and fighter, we may see some truth in her diagnosis—though it seems rather too sinister for the laughing man we've just met.

There have been other manipulators in the hospital, Nurse Ratched remembers, but in the old days (before the improvements the public relations man noted) they could be handled more easily; one Mr. Taber was "an intolerable ward manipulator," but she defeated him. How? We don't know, but her satisfaction in the memory is disturbing. It's clear Nurse Ratched is convinced that anyone who threatens her rule is insane.

The Chief tells us that Nurse Ratched belongs to what he calls the Combine, a shadowy organization that seeks to regulate the world as completely as the Nurse regulates her ward. A combine can mean an organization working against the public interest; its more common usage denotes an agricultural machine. The Chief combines the two meanings of the word and sees the Combine's sinister power in mechanical terms. It's a fantasy, a symptom of his illness, of course—but we'll see that like his fantasies of the hospital, it also contains a great deal of truth about the way the modern world works.

How did Nurse Ratched attain so much power when she is only a nurse? She makes life difficult for doctors, forcing them to quit until she has found one timid enough to obey her. Similarly, she has tested orderly after orderly before locating three who will treat the patients with sufficient hatred.

NOTE: Racism   Some critics of *Cuckoo's Nest* have accused Kesey of racism in his treatment of the black orderlies, who throughout the book are described in unfavorable racial terms. As with the debate over Kesey's treatment of women (more on that later), this is an issue you will have to decide for yourself. Certainly the three aides are the major black characters in the novel, and they are portrayed as despicable people. In Kesey's defense, a valid reason (the rape of his mother) is given for the hatred of one of the aides, nor are any of them above racism themselves—they taunt the Chief for his Indian blood as readily as he taunts them for being black. And other minor black characters—the young girl the Chief meets in the cotton mill, the night aid, Mr. Turkle—are presented sympathetically.

The ward and its morning routine are seen through the Chief's machine-obsessed vision. The orderlies operate on beams of hate; when a patient dies, he shorts out like a broken appliance. Even the walls whirr. Behind her polished windows, the nurse is the machine's invulnerable core; every day she tears off her calendar brings her closer to her goal of complete control of the hospital and the world.

As the patients line up for their medication, we see a flashback to the time when Mr. Taber, the hated manipulator, refused to take the pills Nurse Flinn forces on him. (This seems to be an error on Kesey's part: at the opening of the scene it was implied that Taber left the ward before Nurse Flinn began to work there.) The Chief condenses a lengthy period of time into one scene, as Mr. Taber refuses his pills, hides, is discovered and sedated by the nurse and sexually assaulted by the orderlies, then taken by technicians for electro-shock therapy, and, it's hinted, "brain work"—a lobotomy.

NOTE: *Cuckoo's Nest* **as Comic Strip**   The Chief describes the ward as being "like a cartoon world, where the figures are flat and outlined in black, jerking through some kind of goofy story that might be real funny if it weren't for the cartoon figures being real guys." Here we see Kesey giving us a clue to one of the literary techniques: many critics have pointed out the similarity of *One Flew Over the Cuckoo's Nest* to cartoons and comic strips, in its humor, its fast pace, and most of all in its characters who, as the Chief says, are flat. In outline they may resemble the people we see around us in the real world, but where real people possess a complicated mixture of sympathetic and unsympathetic qualities, flat characters are all good or all bad. They're larger than life, more vivid than life. As he shows us with the Chief's words, and in his description of the technicians as having "cartoon comedy speech," Kesey is well aware of what he's doing. But he lets us know that while his characters may be cartoon-simple, their plight is not cartoon-funny. Punch and Judy puppets may be "beat up by the Devil and swallowed headfirst by a smiling alligator"—but they'll return for the next show. The patients will not get that chance. Their defeat will be final.

After the Chief entertains us with a wild description of the PR man that makes him seem like a rubber toy, he remembers back to a time before he came to the hospital, and we see an example of the forces that make up the Combine. While in high school he toured a California cotton mill; like the hospital it was crammed with machines devoted to efficiency at the expense of human beings. A young black girl flirts with him, then asks him to rescue her from her life in the mill—to rescue her, in effect, from the Combine. But the Chief is powerless to help.

Like the cotton mill, Nurse Ratched's ward is just one small portion of the Combine, a place "for fixing up mistakes made in the neighborhoods and in the schools and in the churches"—places that are themselves segments of the Combine. Now we learn Mr.

Taber's fate. (And because Nurse Ratched classes McMurphy as Taber's equal, we wonder if this is a foreshadowing of McMurphy's fate.) Thanks to his lobotomy, he's no longer a manipulator, no longer an enemy of the Combine. Nor is he like Rucker: the operation has been perfected. Taber is a model citizen; a useful cog in the Combine. Even his death is machinelike, for he runs down after a determined number of years and is embalmed in thirty weight oil, like an auto part. These sorts of deaths are the final dismissal from the hospital ward and from the Combine; they please Nurse Ratched. What doesn't please her is the spirit that McMurphy has carried into the hospital as a new Admission: the spirit of life. The Chief knows she will do her best to destroy it.

SCENE 5

In this long scene we see in more detail how the ward operates. Though the story is still narrated by the Chief, the fog machine is not running at full power, which is to say that the Chief's account of the day's events is mostly straightforwardly true. He can still tune into reality, if he strains. One of these days, he admits, he'll give up and escape into the fog permanently, but this morning he wants to see how McMurphy will react to the ward—another sign that McMurphy may have some role in saving the Chief from his illness.

It's time for the daily Group Meeting. The Nurse leaves her watchful position in the Nurse's Station, and joins the patients in the day room. During the group meetings, patients are encouraged to discuss their problems with each other, under the supervision of Nurse Ratched and Dr. Spivey. Such group therapy is a common psychiatric treatment and often helpful, but in this scene we'll see how the Nurse manipulates the meetings to maintain her control over the patients.

One Chronic, old Pete Bancini, complains as he always does of being tired. The Nurse gets Billy Bibbit to quiet Pete, and then she steers the meeting to a discussion of Dale Harding, the patient who fought McMurphy for the title of Bull Goose Looney. Harding's problems, like those of so many in this book, are in great part sexual: although in scene three we were told he bragged about his wife's desire for him, we now see she apparently thinks him weak and effeminate, and his embarrassment over his lovely, pale hands hints that he fears her judgment is accurate.

McMurphy can't resist disrupting the meeting by making a lewd pun on the meaning of touch. In retaliation, Nurse Ratched reads his psychiatric record, which shows his life to be a mixture of courage, foolhardiness and stupidity. McMurphy beats the Nurse at her own game by joking about his rape conviction, making the doctor smile at his sexual prowess, and by warning the Nurse she had better not continue mispronouncing his name. Though the nurse believes McMurphy is a psycopath (a person whose illness prevents him from feeling any responsibility to family, friends, or society; one who thinks only of his immediate pleasure), Dr. Spivey can't help but be amused. He suggests that McMurphy may be faking mental illness simply to enjoy an easy life at the hospital. In fact, it has become obvious that this probably is McMurphy's intention; when he asks, "Do I look like a sane man?" doctor and reader alike are probably telling themselves, "Yes."

But to Nurse Ratched, anyone who causes her trouble is insane. She insists that the doctor help her regain control of the meeting. As it resumes, McMurphy becomes quiet, puzzled by the lack of laughter among the patients and the Nurse's control over them. Dr. Spivey enthusiastically discusses the theory which governs the ward: the theraputic community. So they will learn how to function in the outside world, the patients are told to discuss their grievances and emotional problems freely with each other, and report on these discussions in the log book. "Our intention," the doctor says, "is to make this as much like your own democratic free neighborhoods as possible—a little world Inside that is a made-to-scale prototype of the big world Outside that you will one day be taking your place in again." The doctor's description of the community contradicts itself—what kind of "democratic free neighborhood" forces citizens to spy on each other? It's easy to see that, despite the democratic facade, the system is rigged to ensure Nurse Ratched's, and the Combine's, control.

As Dr. Spivey talks, the Chief remembers one occasion when the group meeting didn't go as planned. Trying to please Nurse Ratched, the patients competed with each other to see who could confess the most shameful secret, even if they had to invent one. This sick game is interrupted by Pete, the Chronic; his cry of "I'm tired" makes the patients feel ashamed because it represents the truth. Nurse Ratched sends the aides after Pete, but it's a tough fight; a victim of an accident at birth, Pete is too simple-minded to be vulnerable to the Combine. In the Chief's distorted vision, Pete's arm becomes a wrecking ball which exposes the machinery inside the hospital walls. But eventually Nurse Ratched sedates him, and he falls unconscious, never to speak the truth again.

The meeting ends when the doctor grows bored; he is less interested in curing people than in theories, and for this reason, too, he is useful to Nurse Ratched. The patients feel ashamed that once again they have been goaded into attacking one of their own, and McMurphy remains puzzled. He asks Harding if this afternoon's meeting was typical.

Harding is a man who uses his considerable intelligence in unintelligent attempts to deny the truth. Clearly upset by the meeting, he pretends confusion at McMurphy's question. When McMurphy compares the meeting to a pecking party—frenzied chickens pecking each other to death—he sneers that McMurphy doesn't know what he's talking about. Does McMurphy believe he is Freud, Jung, Maxwell Jones? (All three were famous early psychoanalysts.) He speaks the words the public relations man might use: "The staff desires a cure as much as we do. They aren't monsters. Miss Ratched may be a strict middle-aged lady, but she's not some kind of giant monster bent on sadistically pecking out our eyes."

McMurphy is ignorant of psychiatric theory (he mispronounces the famous names Harding has used to impress him), but he insists that the Group Meetings are not going to cure anyone. As for Nurse Ratched pecking out the patients' eyes, McMurphy says she wants to peck at their testicles—just as she's denied her own sexuality, she wants to deny the patients' theirs.

Harding, so upset that his embarrassing hands fly out of control, launches a defense of the Nurse that becomes in our eyes an attack more fierce than any McMurphy has made. "Our Nurse Ratched is a veritable angel of mercy," he announces, but his words are ironic, for each charitable act he describes only proves the Nurse's need for power. She acts on the outside just as she does in the ward.

Now we get a more realistic view of the way the Nurse operates, as McMurphy asks Harding questions we've probably been asking ourselves. How did Nurse Ratched acquire so much power? Doctor Spivey is as timid as his patients, Harding answers, and in this hospital, doctors don't have the authority to hire or fire nurses—that power lies in the hands of a woman who is a friend of Nurse Ratched. And the Nurse's methods of wielding her authority are subtle—without ever making a direct accusation, she can insinuate that the doctor is a morphine addict, that patients have been masturbating, that Harding is a homosexual. Changing McMurphy's metaphor, Harding says the patients aren't chickens but timid cartoon rabbits (looking on, the Chief even sees Billy Bibbit and another patient, Cheswick, become rabbits briefly). They aren't even successful rabbits, for rabbits at least are famed for the sexual abilities the patients sadly lack.

Amazed at Harding's outburst, McMurphy tells him to be quiet. He can't believe that Billy and the other patients are crazy, and he tries to rally them against the nurse. But their fear of Nurse Ratched stops him. Billy again mentions suicide, and Harding explains what happens to troublemakers: they are taken to the Disturbed ward, or subjected to electroshock therapy—which, if they are unlucky, will leave them as ruined as Ellis or Chief Bromden, the latter a victim of more than two hundred treatments.

NOTE: Matriarchy in *Cuckoo's Nest.*   "We are victims of a matriarchy here, my friend," Harding says as he explains Nurse Ratched's reign. A matriarchy is a society where power lies solely in the hands of women; throughout the book we'll see woman who repress and destroy men's sexuality—and in the process destroy their power and freedom as well. This is perhaps the most controversial theme in the book, one that many feminist critics have found highly objectionable. Whether Kesey intended it so or not, it does seem that the Combine is primarily represented by women: Nurse Ratched, Chief Bromden's mother, Billy Bibbit's mother, and (to a lesser extent) Dale Harding's wife, Vera. They rob men of their dignity and manhood; in the Nurse's case, her power is presented in explicitly sexual terms—men can't become sexually aroused by her. If this is Kesey's complete view of women, it is a harsh, unfair one; in his defense, he does have McMurphy specifically stating that not all ball-cutters are women, and, in Scene 6, part one, that sexual repression is only part of a larger problem. There are also secondary female characters—the prostitute, Candy, the girl in the cotton mill, a Japanese-American nurse—who are portrayed sympathetically.

At the end of the discussion, we see how thoroughly the Nurse monitors her patients—she's been listening to and taping every word of the discussion.

But McMurphy thinks he can find a way around the Nurse. If he plays strictly by the ward rules, she can't send him to the Disturbed ward or for electroshock therapy. If he can anger her without violating any rules, he will win. As a gambling man, he wants to make the contest more interesting by taking bets on the outcome. He's cocky, confident of his success. Harding and the other Acutes place bets, but Harding throws cold water on McMurphy by reminding him, "You won't be going anyplace for awhile."

SCENE 6

The scene opens with an example of the black humor (humor also marked by the grotesque and the ironic) that we'll see often in the book. The Chief remembers one Christmas when Santa Claus visited the ward. It's likely the intruder was just a fat old man with a red nose, but in the Chief's remembrance he represents the generous spirit of Christmas, and as he is nabbed by the aides and imprisoned, (to leave six years later "clean-shaven and skinny as a pole") we wonder: if the hospital can destroy even Christmas, how can anything good survive?

Through the Chief's warped vision we see the control the Nurse maintains over the ward. She even masters time, occasionally making it go so fast that the view out the window turns from morning to night in seconds, then slowing it to a snail's pace. She likes to speed things up to make pleasant activities pass more quickly, and slow things down for unpleasant events, like the death of a patient next to the Chief. Of course the Chief is describing a familiar phenomenon—bad times seem to pass more slowly than good—but his "untrue" description reminds us of a deeper truth.

Today is different, though, because McMurphy is there. Time moves at a normal pace; even the fog is gone. Nurse Ratched's shift ends and another nurse arrives, and McMurphy plays cards with the patients. When he complains about the music being piped into the room, threatening to turn it off, he's warned that causing trouble will make him forfeit his bet. Meanwhile, the comparison of the piped music to a waterfall causes the Chief to remember a waterfall near the Indian village where he grew up: again, his memories of his Indian youth are clear and precise compared to his fog-shrouded present. (We'll see, too, the eventual—and important—fate of that waterfall.)

As the Chief describes McMurphy playing cards, we receive additional insights into the new patient's character. He brags about his skill at the game, hamming it up like a riverboat gambler. But after a string of victories, he arranges to lose all his winnings. The patients understand what he's done, but they're still pleased: McMurphy's generosity has given them a little self-respect.

Now it is time for the patients to take their sleeping pills, but McMurphy disrupts this routine, too: the sight of him scares the night nurse into dropping pills and spilling water, and in the confusion, McMurphy is able to hide some of the drugs in his palm. As a result, the Chief for the first time in years will go to bed without being under the influence of sedating drugs. Just as important, McMurphy tricks the Chief into revealing that he isn't deaf and dumb: he can at least hear.

NOTE: The Use of Symbols   As McMurphy undresses, we see his shorts—black satin covered with white whales. He tells Chief Bromden the shorts come "from a co-ed at Oregon State, Chief, a literary major. She gave them to me because she said I was a symbol." A symbol, in literature, is a person or object that stands both for itself and for something else—another person, another object, an idea. For example, in the descriptions of the electro-shock therapy, the focus on the cross-shaped table and the electric crown of thorns are intended to symbolize Christ's crucifixion: the patients undergoing treatment there are in some way similar to Christ in their innocence and their suffering. And more elaborate symbolism specifically linking McMurphy to Christ comes at the end of the book. Now we're given another clear example of a symbol: the undershorts McMurphy is wearing are intended to remind you of Herman Melville's classic American novel, *Moby Dick* (itself a work of symbolism more complex than anything in *Cuckoo's Nest*), in which Captain Ahab chases an enormous white whale at the eventual cost of his ship and his life. Is McMurphy like the obsessed captain? Like the whale—a force of nature that can never be captured or known? Or is Kesey having a joke on literary majors and professors who spend too much time looking for symbols and who take them too seriously when they find them? After all, the whales are not real whales, just images on a pair of silly undershorts. McMurphy may sometimes resemble Captain Ahab, Moby-Dick, even Christ—but it's wise to remember that first and foremost he is McMurphy.

SCENE 7

Without his medication, the Chief sleeps restlessly, enduring a series of nightmares. The flow of bizarre sights reveals much about the Chief's life, and when, at the end of the scene he asks of them, "But if they don't exist, how can a man see them?" the answer is, they *do* exist: they are the truth, even if they didn't happen.

The Chief envisions the hospital as a tremendous machine that hums like a dam—and we'll see later that a hydroelectric dam played a cruel part in triggering the Chief's illness. Workers with waxen faces grab a Chronic patient, Blastic (whom we saw the orderlies abusing in Scene 4), hang him on a hook that dangles from the ceiling, and scalp him—the bared, opened skull revealing only the rust and ashes of a ruined machine, another of the Combine's errors. As the fog rolls in, the Chief glimpses the public relations man, laced into a woman's corset so tight it bloats his face— like so many in this book, he has denied his true sexuality. From the corset stays dangle what seem at first to be more scalps, but what are actually male genitals, reminders of McMurphy's warning of what the Nurse and the hospital want to do to the patients.

The Chief is comforted by Mr. Turkle, one of the few kindly aides in the hospital. Aides and doctors take the dead Mr. Blastic away, giving his body more care than they ever showed the living man.

SCENE 8

The Chief awakens the next morning, surprised that McMurphy is up before him, even more surprised that the new patient is singing. In this ward, songs are like laughter, never heard. The tunes McMurphy sings aren't given titles (they are American folk songs, "The Wagoner's Lad" and "The Roving Gambler"), but their lyrics show a man refusing to be tied down by a woman—exactly the situation McMurphy finds himself in now.

The Chief wonders why the Combine hasn't defeated McMurphy before this, and he speculates that the newcomer moved around too often to be snared. He thinks, too, that McMurphy may have survived by not caring about anyone, in a sense, agreeing with Nurse Ratched's diagnosis of him as a psychopath. We'll see later whether the Chief is correct.

Now, at this early hour, McMurphy is forced into the first of his battles with the hospital. He wants to brush his teeth, but the toothpaste is locked up until 6:45, McMurphy is amazed—why is toothpaste being guarded like a dangerous weapon? The aide answers in the way bureaucrats always answer: it's policy. The aide asks, "What do you s'pose it'd be like if evahbody was to brush their teeth whenever they took a notion to brush?"

In fact, this question doesn't seem completely absurd; some of the patients we've met in this ward might well decide to brush their teeth twenty-four hours a day. But McMurphy makes the question, and the aide, appear ridiculous, and he resourcefully defeats the aide by brushing his teeth with soap power. Angered by McMurphy, the aide takes his wrath out on Chief Bromden: the usual pattern in the hospital.

NOTE: On laughter   Here again we're reminded of the power of laughter. The Chief looks at McMurphy and recalls his father, who also could defeat people with jokes. He remembers a scene with his father talking to white visitors who want him to sign a contract—we'll find out later what that contract entails and its effect on the Chief's tribe. The Chief's father makes fun of the visitors by pretending to be just the man they think he is, an ignorant, superstitious savage. He tells them he can see geese (note the choice of bird), though it's July and geese would not be migrating then in the skies of Oregon. Annoyed at being made fun of, the visitors leave. "I forget sometimes what laughter can do," the Chief says; it's McMurphy who has enabled him to remember.

Nurse Ratched arrives and the aide bested by McMurphy over the toothpaste is so anxious to tattle he forgets the truly important news—that Mr. Blastic has died. In this hospital, violations of the rules cause more concern than the deaths of the patients.

McMurphy has resumed singing, angering the
Nurse. Again the Chief sees her rage as a physical
force that transforms her from a human being into a
machine—this time a huge diesel truck with a radiator
grill smile, rolling full speed towards McMurphy. But
McMurphy stops her by walking casually from the
latrine wearing only a towel.

He explains that someone has taken his work farm
clothing (using a criminal's word—boosted for sto-
len—language that the Nurse doesn't understand).
When Nurse Ratched realizes that this reasonable
explanation of his nakedness has made her seem silly
she takes out her anger (now compared to a blizzard)
on the aides. Then McMurphy drops his towel,
revealing that he was not naked but had been wearing
his gaudy undershorts.

It's a complete defeat for Nurse Ratched: only as
other patients straggle out of their beds does she
regain her self-control. Even then the anger hasn't dis-
appeared; we can still see it in her greetings to the
patients, pleasant-sounding on the surface, but
barbed and cutting underneath. She warns Fredrickson and Sefelt about switching their medication, tells
Billy not to disappoint his mother, asks Harding about
the chewed fingernails on his embarrassing hands.
No weakness escapes her. She'd like to use the same
tactics on McMurphy, but he's still singing.

Chief Bromden continues to sweep after everyone
has left. At the end of the scene, as he sweeps under
the patients' beds, we see the contrast between the
world of the hospital and McMurphy's world—or,
actually, we smell the contrast. The hospital's smells
are musty, depressing; McMurphy's bed has "the
man smell of dust and dirt from the open fields, and
sweat, and work," the true smells of a life not con-
trolled by the Combine.

SCENE 9

Our second morning in the ward is much different from our first. McMurphy is doing everything he can to liven things up, inventing stories about Billy Bibbit's sexual adventures (again, sex is as necessary as laughter to a healthy life), and acting as if there was no place on earth he'd rather be than this hospital with its fine beds and good food. He refuses to take the rules seriously: even the clock, which with Nurse Ratched's assistance rules the ward, becomes a butter-smeared victim of McMurphy's pranks.

But the Big Nurse is still in control. When McMurphy asks her to dampen the piped-in music, or let patients use a quieter room for their card games, she dismisses his requests as impossible and selfish. Her answers make a certain sense—almost all of Nurse Ratched's rules do. She is never on the surface, an irrational woman. But because she demands obedience at the expense of charity and generosity, she becomes irrational, a monster. The tension between the Nurse and the new patient is growing. "Everyone on the ward can feel it's started."

McMurphy leaves to be interviewed by Doctor Spivey. At the group meeting we learn that he's cleverly used the interview to maneuver his way around Nurse Ratched. Before the nurse even has a chance to begin the "pecking party," (note how she claims they were making "quite a bit of headway with Mr. Harding's problem" the day before, when of course just the opposite was true), McMurphy takes over. He's convinced the doctor that the ward should hold a carnival. Taber, the other trouble maker, once made the same request, and nothing came of it. As soon as the Nurse trains her eyes on the doctor, we see the project is doomed this time, too.

But McMurphy isn't finished. He has also figured out a way to obtain his card room by cleverly using the Nurse's own arguments against her. Since the music must be turned up loud enough for the patients to hear it, why not turn it up still louder? Then why not open another room to give other patients a quiet place to read?

This time the doctor can't be pressured to oppose McMurphy's plan. The Nurse is so angry at McMurphy's victory she can't read her notes for the group meeting. McMurphy prevents the pecking party from starting by monopolizing the discussion. Dream analysis is a frequently used technique in therapy, but he makes it seem absurd by inventing a dream about his father and using the dream as an excuse to tell tall tales about his past life.

Despite this victory, Chief Bromden looks on and grows discouraged again. Nurse Ratched still covers "one whole side of the room like a Jap statue" (presumably an enormous Buddha). "She lost a little battle here today, but it's a minor battle in a big war that she's been winning and that she'll go on winning." Why? Because she is with the Combine, and the Combine can afford to lose a few battles. It never gives up, and eventually its opponents always surrender. These thoughts are so depressing that the Chief escapes them by hiding in his fog, the fog that gives him safety at the expense of sanity.

SCENE 10

A few days later we see McMurphy continuing to plot his war against the Big Nurse. The patients are playing Monopoly, which, given their mental confusion, becomes a hectic and, for the reader, very funny game. Martini, for example, sees more pieces on the board than actually exist, places hotels on properties where hotels don't belong, and rolls imaginary dice. Yet here, too, McMurphy shows a relaxed generosity, counting out Martini's moves so that Martini invariably lands on the single property he owns. Again, we see it's sometimes necessary to bend the rules to help people.

SCENE 11

McMurphy has emerged victorious from the battle of the toothpaste and the battle of the card room. Now begins the battle of the World Series, which becomes the focus for the rest of Part I. In this scene we see that the hospital is beginning to wear McMurphy down, and the reason is not just the Nurse or the staff, but the patients, too, for they lack McMurphy's courage.

McMurphy has planned to watch the World Series even though the games won't be shown during the ward's scheduled television time. The Nurse, of course, says he can't watch the Series, a refusal that doesn't surprise McMurphy one bit. What does surprise him is the patients' complete agreement with her. Rules must always be followed. During the group meeting, only Cheswick, a would-be rebel happy at last to have an ally, backs McMurphy up.

McMurphy is disgusted at the patients' cowardice. Billy Bibbit attempts to explain it but can't. We learn that Nurse Ratched has spoiled McMurphy's blackjack games by first stopping the patients from playing for money, then by locking away the cigarettes they'd been betting with instead. The routine that McMurphy disrupted is reasserting itself.

When McMurphy mentions the World Series again, Harding makes fun of him, so angering McMurphy that he starts discussing ways of breaking out of the hospital. The strong-windows can't be broken with wooden chairs or tables; a bed is too big to be used. Only the control panel in the tub room would work, and at 400 pounds it's too heavy to be lifted. But McMurphy is mad enough to give it a try, and he makes a bet he'll succeed. He strains; for a second the doubters fall quiet as it seems he might win. But he isn't strong enough; he loses his bet, winning only the satisfaction of knowing he made the attempt. Here is another example of foreshadowing: later in the book we'll see another bet involving this control panel (which is a symbol of the Combine's power), and another try at using it to gain freedom.

SCENE 12

This brief scene points up the contrast between the world of nature and the wilderness (which is associated with the Chief's childhood and with McMurphy), and the drab, regulated world of the hospital. As the Chief sweeps the staff room, where a visiting doctor talks to the residents, he stares at a painting hanging on the wall. It shows a wilderness scene: a fisherman (just as the Chief's tribe were fishermen), an aspen grove, white mountain peaks, a world so alluring that the Chief imagines he can enter it and from an aspen-shaded perch stare back at the hospital behind him. This art work is one of the improvements that makes the hospital a better place than the old one. "Why, a man that would want to run away from a place as nice as this, why there'd be something wrong with him," says the public relations man. But how much of an improvement is it really? The painting is still merely a painting, an artificial vision of a free and beautiful world to soothe people locked in an ugly one. Indeed, at the end of the scene, even the visiting doctor seems lost and unhappy, hugging himself as if for him, too, the world of the painting, however unreal, was preferable to the world of the hospital.

SCENES 13 AND 14

The first of these two short scenes reminds us that it is always easier not to be brave; the Chief knows there is safety hiding in the fog, a fact that McMurphy hasn't yet realized. But the second scene undercuts the Chief's faith in the safety the fog provides: against the Combine, safety is always temporary. Old Rawler, the Disturbed patient we heard in scene eleven, has killed himself by cutting off his testicles. In effect, he's done the job the Combine had already begun. The Chief wonders why he took the touble: "All the guy had to do was wait."

SCENE 15

This scene forms the climax of Part I: the fiercest battle yet between McMurphy and Nurse Ratched. It begins with Chief Bromden discussing the fog machine that clouds his view of the hospital. To him, this imaginary device is identical to a real device used when he was a soldier in World War II. Fog was blown over English airfields to protect them from German bombers; as you stepped out onto the runway, "You were safe from the enemy, but you were awfully alone." When you did meet someone, you saw him with terrifying clarity: "You didn't want to look at his face and he didn't want to look at yours, because it's painful to see somebody so clear that it's like looking inside him, but then neither did you want to look away and lose him completely. You had a choice: you could either strain and look at things that appeared in

front of you in the fog, painful as it might be, or you
could relax and lose yourself."

And we understand that those are the choices the
Chief faces in his life in the hospital. He can try to see
things as they are, even when they're painful and
dangerous. Or he can lose himself in the safety of the
fog. Right now the fog is winning. The Chief has
learned how to cope with it; before, it panicked him
and sent him into the Shock Shop. Now he's used to
illness, and he knows that if he just gives into it, no
one will bother him. "Being lost isn't so bad."

Lately the fog has been thicker than usual, thanks
to the disturbances McMurphy has caused. The Chief
says the fog machine has been turned on more frequently, but we're familiar enough with his illness
(the fog rolls in when he's frightened, disappears
when he's calm) that we understand that McMurphy
has caused a disturbance within the Chief: McMurphy is a constant reminder that there is a world of
danger, but also of freedom, outside the hospital.

The Group Meeting begins with Billy Bibbit under
discussion. We see the problems his stuttering has
caused him. Notice that the first word he stuttered
was Mama—another signal of the destructive power
of the matriarchy.

Lost in the fog, the Chief sees glimpses of the other
patients around him, just as he once bumped into
other soldiers on the fogged-in airfield. He meets Colonel Matterson, an ancient Army officer who speaks
what at first seems like utter craziness. "The flag is . . .
Ah-mer-ica. America . . . is the plum. The peach. The
watermelon. . . . Mexico is . . . the wal-nut . . . Mexico
is . . . the rainbow." With the clarity the fog gives him,
the Chief now understands that the colonel's words
made sense. Like the Chief himself, he speaks things
that are true even if they didn't happen: the truth of

metaphor, of poetry. But the fog that gives this brief moment of perception then steals it away. The Colonel disappears, perhaps for good.

Patients float by, Pete, Billy Bibbit, whose chances for love were spoiled by his mother, others. The Chief is powerless to help them, for the moment you try to help someone you become vulnerable yourself. The Chief is on the verge of being lost for good. "I'm further off than I've ever been." He'll become one of the Vegetables, like Ellis or Ruckley. As he drifts towards that fate, he remembers the forces that sent him to the hospital in the first place: the war, his tribal village's destruction by a government gravel crusher, his father's aging.

Then, suddenly, a voice breaks through: McMurphy. "He's still trying to pull people out of the fog," the Chief says. "Why don't he leave me be?" McMurphy is arguing about watching the World Series. He wants a new vote. This time a few of the patients have been impressed enough by McMurphy's attempt to lift the control panel, and are annoyed enough at Nurse Ratched that they back him up. As the vote is taken, the Chief imagines that McMurphy's red, work-strong hand is pulling each Acute out of the fog to stand with him.

McMurphy wins the votes of everyone who took part in the election, all twenty Acutes. In any true democracy that should give him a victory. But the Nurse goes by her own rules, which say that McMurphy requires a majority of everyone in the ward, including the Chronics who are incapable of understanding an election. He needs twenty one votes.

McMurphy begs one Chronic after another for help. Ruckley, Ellis, Pete, Colonel Matterson, George: none of them is willing. Then he approaches the Chief. Just as he was that first morning when McMurphy wanted to shake his hand, the Chief is terrified. He wants to be left undisturbed in the fog.

Nevertheless, as McMurphy stands over him (notice how the Chief distorts their heights: McMurphy is shorter than the Indian and could never stand "over" him), the Chief feels his hand raising. At first he blames the act on McMurphy, as if he were like the Nurse, able to control people by hidden wires. Then he admits, "No, that's not the truth. I lifted it myself." While Nurse Ratched uses her power to force people to do what *she* wants, McMurphy's power is that he gives people the courage to do what *they* want. With McMurphy's help, the Chief has pulled himself out of the fog: a defeat for the Combine. But the angry Nurse announces that the voting is closed. There will be no World Series.

The Nurse watches from her glassed-in Nurse's Station as the Acutes perform their assigned chores. McMurphy's grinning irritates her, and her irritation grows when he tosses down his rag and goes to the television and turns it on to the baseball game. The Nurse switches off the set from the control room. But just as he did with the toothpaste, McMurphy turns defeat into victory by ignoring the Nurse's action. He doesn't move. He stares at the blank screen as if the World Series could be seen on it.

The Nurse can't tolerate this behavior. She comes close to losing control. And now the other patients, Harding, Cheswick, Billy and the rest, sit down with McMurphy to watch the non-existent game. Nurse Ratched is screaming. Says the Chief, "If somebody'd of come in and took a look, men watching a blank TV, a fifty year-old woman hollering and squealing at the back of their heads about discipline and order and recriminations, they'd of thought the whole bunch was crazy as loons." Ironically, by acting crazy,

McMurphy and the men have shown that they are
sane. By clinging to her rules past the point where
they make sense, the Nurse has sunk to the patients'
level and below.

PART II

Part II of *One Flew Over the Cuckoo's Nest* consists of
eight scenes.

SCENE 1

We're still in the day room, with the patients seated
around the switched-off television, just as they were
at the end of Part I. Why did Kesey choose to split
things up this way—stick this intermission in the
middle of what might easily be a single scene?
Because we're in another world. On the surface nothing has changed; underneath everything has. The
patients have asserted themselves; Nurse Ratched has
lost control. Now she's the one being watched—and
not just by the patients, but by her staff, who for the
first time see that she, too, is vulnerable.

Still, this scene shows that the change is not as complete as it first seems. McMurphy has scored an
encouraging victory, but we've already seen that the
Nurse and the Combine can afford a few losses.

Indeed, the Chief fears that his situation is more
dangerous since McMurphy pulled him out of the
fog. His immediate worry: Nurse Ratched and the
staff will guess that he is not deaf and dumb. One of
the aides seems to suspect the truth and tries to trick
the chief into revealing it for certain, though without
success.

Even before the incident with the television, Nurse
Ratched had scheduled a meeting of the hospital staff
to discuss McMurphy. The Chief's descriptions of

past meetings make them sound brutal; his hallucinations transform the bitterness displayed by the staff members into poison and acid, and the discussions of the patients are so lengthy the men being discussed appear to materialize on the coffee table, naked and "vulnerable to any fiendish notion" the staff took.

As Nurse Ratched enters, the Chief worries that, like the aide, she suspects his secret and will want to investigate further. He's so nervous he's ready to confess but is saved when the Nurse herself becomes rattled by the stares of the staff members who have learned of her defeat.

The meeting begins. Originally Nurse Ratched called it to arrange McMurphy's move into the Disturbed Ward; Dr. Spivey believes this is still her goal, and he agrees that given McMurphy's recent behavior, she may be correct. He asks the young residents (physicians past their internships but still in training) for their opinion.

Ironically, the doctors, though educated and intelligent, show no more courage than do their patients. They, too, are afraid, and fear makes them act like sheep, each agreeing unthinkingly with the other, each trying to outdo the other in the use of impressive-sounding but meaningless psychological terms. When one resident dares to suggest the truth—that McMurphy isn't mentally ill—the rest attack him: it's another pecking party. Finally all agree that he is a negative oedipal (a diagnosis chosen seemingly at random) and that he should be moved to the Disturbed Ward.

This, however, is no longer what Nurse Ratched wants. She wants revenge, though of course her explanation makes it appear that she is only acting for the good of the other patients. If she permits McMurphy to be moved to the Disturbed Ward, he will appear a martyr who has sacrificed himself for the other patients. If, on the other hand, Nurse Ratched can keep him in her ward, she'll be able to prove that he is just a selfish, fearful, ordinary man. She'll have ample opportunity to break him, she reminds everyone: McMurphy has been committed to the hospital, and she and the other staff members are the ones who decide when he will be released.

SCENE 2

McMurphy, unaware that Nurse Ratched has planned a counterattack, acts more outrageously than ever. Made to clean the latrine, he writes obscenities in reversed letters to shock the Nurse when she checks his job with a mirror. And he is not the only one being difficult. The other patients have slacked off on their chores, preferring to listen to McMurphy's stories. So strong is the new patient's personality that even the Chief, who heard the Nurse's plotting, hopes that McMurphy can defeat her and the Combine.

How did McMurphy become so strong? This is the question the Chief asks himself as he looks in the mirror. He has spent much of his life trying to be on the inside the same man he looks to be on the outside world: strong, hard, and mean. He's never succeeded. Maybe, the Chief thinks, McMurphy has survived because "he hadn't let what he looked like run his life one way or the other." The Chief may feel weaker than his face appears, and Harding may be ashamed of his feminine hands, but McMurphy is secure enough that he doesn't always have to act like the roughneck he appears to be. He can paint; he can write letters in lovely script.

You'll notice how clearly the Chief is thinking here. Even though it is the other Acute patients who seem to be most obviously changed by McMurphy's arrival, the changes that McMurphy brought about in the Chief are more profound. The fog machine has been shut down. The hallucinations will still disturb him, but much less frequently; in general, for the rest of the book, the Chief's descriptions of events will match what we would see if we were with him. When he wakes up at night, he sees not machine and scalp-hunting aides, but the real world outside his window.

The view surprises him. The smell of autumn recalls time's passage, his Indian boyhood. Far below he spots a young dog happily sniffing around the hospital grounds for squirrel holes. (Compare this dog to the one the Chief described in Scene 1, Part I, afraid and lost in the fog; it's another sign of the Chief's healing.) The dog freezes as a flock of Canadian geese fly in V formation across the sky.

NOTE: Images of Freedom   Unlike McMurphy's whale-dotted shorts, the symbols here are not jokes. The dog and the geese in flight are images of freedom—the freedom of the Chief's Indian past, the freedom McMurphy has brought into the ward as Bull Goose Looney. What will happen to this freedom? The answer is unclear, but not encouraging. For the geese fly away, and as the dog chases after them, his chase leads him towards a highway and into the path of an oncoming car—another of the machines the Combine uses to subdue the wilderness. The Chief is taken away before he learns the dog's fate.

The Chief looks at the nurse who led him to bed. In what is not a hallucination but simply an act of imagination, he sees her at home trying to scrub her wine-colored birthmark away. You may remember that McMurphy, too, has a "wine-colored scar"—we saw it in Part I, Scene 3—but his is healing. The nurse's mark can't be healed because it rises from the illness inside her, both the cause and a symptom of her hatred. Against so much hatred, the Chief feels himself weakening. He wants McMurphy's help, but McMurphy is not awake to offer it.

SCENE 3

We're back at the group meeting, but what a difference between this one and those that have come before it! Now McMurphy isn't alone in squabbling with Nurse Ratched; other patients—especially Cheswick, who no longer backs down now that he sees an ally beside him—do so too.

The one question McMurphy has is why the Big Nurse has given up so easily. On a trip to the swimming pool he learns the truth. She hasn't given up; she's merely biding her time. While the Chief nervously stays at McMurphy's side (Chief Bromden's fear of water is another sign of his decline since his Indian youth), McMurphy talks to the pool lifeguard, an ex-football player now in the Disturbed ward. When McMurphy says he likes the hospital more than the work farm he was at previously, the lifeguard disagrees. At least at the work farm you know you'll be released at the end of your sentence. Patients committed to the hospital don't have a set sentence: they can be held for as long as the hospital wants to hold them.

The Chief remembers what the Nurse said at the staff meeting and is afraid, and we can see McMurphy becoming afraid, too. As the patients leave the pool, a group from another ward arrives; one of them, severely handicapped, falls on the wet floor. Harding and Cheswick go to help him, and they ask for McMurphy's assistance. McMurphy refuses. He won't help anyone for fear that it might endanger his chances of being released.

The next day we see further evidence of his new attitude. He obediently cleans the latrine. When Cheswick attacks the Nurse at Group Meeting, McMurphy declines to back him up, so upsetting Cheswick that he is marched off to the Disturbed Ward. The Nurse is regaining her power. For the first time in days the Chief suffers a hallucination—again he sees the Combine's machinery of control and says "It beams all the way into my stomach."

At first the Acutes believe McMurphy's obedience is a new tactic he's using against Nurse Ratched. The Chief knows better. McMurphy is finally getting cagey, just as the Chief's father finally realized it would be smarter to allow the government to buy his tribal village. (The government will build a hydroelectric dam that will destroy the waterfall the Chief has already described; because the Indians spear salmon as they leap up the falls, the dam will effectively destroy the tribe's livelihood.) Like hiding in the fog, giving in is the safest, smartest thing to do.

Eventually the Acutes see the truth about McMurphy. He is no more courageous than they are; Nurse Ratched was right. The other patients seem to be resigned to this truth, even Cheswick. But McMurphy has inspired hope, and when he takes that hope away he leaves the patients worse off than before. Cheswick, who had waited so long for an ally, can't endure life when that ally surrenders to the enemy. At the next trip to the swimming pool, he drowns himself.

SCENE 4

This relatively short scene focuses on two Acutes, Sefelt and Fredrickson, whose situation makes McMurphy re-think his own. Sefelt suffers a severe epileptic seizure, which Nurse Ratched says was caused by his refusal to take his medication.

Sefelt's friend Fredrickson, who, like Cheswick, talks tough then gives up, argues with Nurse Ratched. She says she can't understand why Sefelt hasn't been taking his Dilantin—a medication that suppresses seizures. In fact, she is being coy: she and everyone else know that Sefelt gives his dose to Fredrickson. Sefelt is afraid that the medication will make him grow old, and Fredrickson is afraid of seizures. They both give in to their fears.

As usual, Fredrickson backs down. When McMurphy asks why Sefelt is afraid to take the Dilantin, Fredrickson opens his mouth as an answer. The Dilantin rots gums. On the other hand, if he doesn't take the drug, he will damage his teeth by gritting them during a seizure like the one Sefelt suffered. "Hell of a life," comments Scanlon, who is observing. "Damned if you do and damned if you don't." McMurphy realizes that he is in the same bind: disobedience may not have done him any good, but will obedience save him?

SCENE 5

This very short scene shows that Nurse Ratched has so successfully crushed McMurphy's revolt that everything is back to normal. The Chief may not be wrapped in fog, but the machinery within the walls, quiet after McMurphy's victory, is once again humming.

SCENE 6

McMurphy's fear and puzzlement have grown worse, and so have the Chief's. While the patients are in the library, an aide announces that Harding's wife has come to visit. This is the woman Harding claims "can't get enough of him," but of whom he is terrified.

Vera Harding is a more complicated character than many of the other women in the book. In some ways she is a member of the Nurse's matriarchy, at least in the sexual fear she inspires in her husband. But far from repressing her own sexuality, she's exaggerated it—in fact, it's hinted that she's able to visit the ward outside normal visiting hours by promising sexual favors to the aide. Still, her effect on Harding is crushing. He grows nervous, he talks too much in his over-intellectual way, and his hands flutter so wildly he is unable to light her cigarette. As he makes fun of her bad grammar, she makes fun of his laugh and complains about his effeminate friends.

McMurphy is caught in the middle of the argument, Vera flirting with him, Harding seeking to have him on his side. When Harding asks McMurphy what he thinks of his wife, McMurphy explodes. "I know what you want me to think; you want me to feel sorry for you, to think she's a real bitch. Well, you didn't make her feel like any queen either."

This is an accurate analysis of Harding's relationship with his wife. Vera is not a monstrous Nurse Ratched; in some ways she is a victim herself. But it's clear McMurphy is not angry with Harding. He's discovering the trap he's caught in, a trap that is giving him bad dreams. Obedience to the Combine has not helped him at all. When Martini plays with the unused control panel in the tub room, pretending to see people strapped into it, it's a sign of healing—like the Chief, Martini is beginning to notice that his hallucinations are hallucinations, and even to joke about them. But McMurphy is too disturbed to notice the improvement; too disturbed even to laugh—a dangerous sign.

SCENE 7

Three weeks after the revolt over the TV, the patients, firmly under the Nurse's control, are taken for tuberculosis exams. (The Chief sees it as "a check to see if everybody's machinery is functioning up to par.") Next to the x-ray room is the Shock Shop, where the electro-shock therapy takes place. McMurphy asks Harding to explain the therapy, and Harding in his clever way does. Electricity is shot through the brain; the treatment, destructive to brain cells, is generally out of fashion, Nurse Ratched being one of the few who still use it. (Harding's mention of "the grand old Faulknerian tradition . . . brain burning" is a joke; among William Faulkner's most famous short stories is one entitled "Barn Burning.") Harding explains that, like lobotomy, electro-shock therapy has its advantages: it's cheap and painless. But a technique developed by striking cattle on the head with sledgehammers certainly seems brutal when applied to humans.

McMurphy is upset and afraid. He's discovered that the game he's been playing is for much higher stakes than he imagined. Not only may he not be allowed to leave, he may end up on the shock table— and Nurse Ratched is the one who will decide his fate.

The patients discuss whether or not their problems are entirely the fault of Nurse Ratched, and they agree she alone is responsible. But McMurphy says the Nurse is only part of a bigger problem, one that he can't yet explain. The Chief believes that McMurphy has stumbled on to the secret of the Combine. In a sense, the Chief is correct. McMurphy may not believe in the Chief's fantasy of all-powerful machines, but he's beginning to understand the truth that underlies that fantasy—that Nurse Ratched is only one representative of the forces of fear that control too much of modern society. And those forces are not just sexually repressive—if that were the case all he would have to do is rape Nurse Ratched to defeat her. But that wouldn't solve anything, he knows. All he can do is try to avoid the Nurse entirely.

Harding is amused. McMurphy in turn accuses Harding and the others of using him to win privileges they've been afraid to fight for themselves. He says he has just as much to lose from disobedience as they do.

Now, a revelation. "No," Harding tells McMurphy. "You've got more to lose than I do, my friend." For Harding and most of the other Acutes are not committed but have placed themselves in the hospital voluntarily. Unlike McMurphy, they can leave whenever they want.

McMurphy is dumbfounded. Why would Billy and the rest stay in such a place when they could been enjoying the freedom of the outside world? They aren't so bad off: McMurphy has known many unhospitalized people with more severe problems.

Billy tries to explain. They don't want to be here, he says, but they're too weak. They're not like McMurphy. They don't have his guts. Billy breaks down in tears.

NOTE: McMurphy is coming to understand the patients' problems. Their weakness comes not so much from their illnesses as from the fear planted in them by society and by the hospital, and he sees that he himself has become a victim of this fear, too. You can see him struggling to make sense of this problem, preparing for the confrontation that comes in the next scene.

SCENE 8

Like the final scene of Part I, the final scene of Part II shows McMurphy in full battle against Nurse Ratched.

McMurphy is upset by what Harding has told him. Chief Bromden compares him to a dog (like the dog in scene two, Part Two), worrying at a hole and wondering if he should fight or play it safe. But McMurphy has already been playing it safe, and what good has it done him? Like Sefelt, he's damned either way.

On the return from the x-ray room, he asks the aide to let him go to the canteen and buy cigarettes. (These cigarettes, we remember—and we'll be reminded by Fredrickson at the group meeting—are not given directly to the patient but are dispatched to the Nurse's Station and doled out from there.) Chief Bromden knows something is about to happen, and he gets excited. The impatient, ear-ringing feeling reminds him of the minutes before a high school football game.

At this afternoon's group meeting, the epileptic Mr. Sefelt is the topic for discussion. As always, Nurse Ratched aims at his weakest point—his fear of getting old. The Chief notices that McMurphy appears different than he's appeared lately, no longer slouched but flushed and reckless-looking.

Nurse Ratched, confident of her complete control, announces from within her glass Nurse's Station (behind its windows she looks like a mechanical fortune teller) that the patients must be punished for their disobedience of three weeks before. She is closing the tub room where the card games are held.

No one says anything. The patients wait to see how McMurphy will react to this attack on his earliest improvement to the ward. At first McMurphy seems not to have noticed what the Nurse has said. But the Chief realizes that something is up. As McMurphy walks towards the Nurse's Station, "he was the logger again, the swaggering gambler, the big, redheaded brawling Irishman, the cowboy out of the TV set walking down the middle of the street to meet a dare." Nurse Ratched, frightened, looks for help. But McMurphy doesn't attack her directly. Instead he stops in front of the Nurse's Station, which with its polished windows and control panel is a symbol of all the power the Nurse and the Combine possess. Then he shatters the window—claiming that he wanted to get one of the cigarettes he bought that morning, and that the Nurse had made her patients scrub the glass so thoroughly he didn't notice the window was even there.

McMurphy is back in action. The football game the Chief was waiting for has begun, the ringing in his head has stopped.

PART III

Part III consists of two scenes.

SCENE 1

McMurphy has returned with all his power to disrupt the Nurse's world, but for the moment she is not fighting back; she realizes that time will always be on her side. Meanwhile, McMurphy is making her life as difficult as he can. He forms a basketball team and in one game knocks an aide in the nose. He writes requests, ruining the Nurse's pen in the process, plants more obscene notes in the latrine, spoils her attempt to make the patients spy on each other by writing false stories about himself in her log book. When the window of the Nurse's Station is at last replaced, he breaks it again. What's more, the other Acutes are following his example.

McMurphy's next plan is to take a fishing trip. He and the other members of the ward will be accompanied by two "aunts" from Portland. Nurse Ratched, of course, opposes the idea; far from seeing its value as therapy, she sees the trip only as a threat to her control. To retain that control, she tries to destroy the patients' growing self-confidence, telling them repeatedly of the ocean's dangers. McMurphy turns her words against her: the roughness of the sea will be exhilarating; where she sees perils to fear he sees challenges to master. But she will have none of it.

The Nurse's warnings succeed in scaring many of the patients, and it seems McMurphy may not get enough passengers to pay for the boat trip. Though he has no money, the Chief would like to go. But he fears that signing up will be an admission that he isn't deaf and dumb; once that discovery was made, Nurse Ratched might be angry enough at his deception to make him deaf and dumb for real. Another of the ironies of life in the hospital: "I had to keep on acting deaf if I wanted to hear at all." In this strange world, to protect what you are, you may have to pretend to be the opposite.

The Chief lies in his bed thinking of the many years of his deception. It was, he says, other people "who first started acting like I was too dumb to hear or see or say anything at all." Because he was an Indian, people assumed he was stupid. He remembers when, at age ten, he saw a car pull up to his house in the Indian village. The visitors aren't tourists, he knows, and they haven't come to buy fish, for tourists and shoppers are too frightened of Indians to venture so near.

Out of the car step two men and a woman, the woman, like Nurse Ratched, dressed in an outfit stiff as armor. They're looking for Chief Bromden's father, because they want to discuss with him the government's plans (the plans being the destruction of the village for a hydroelectric dam).

The young boy gets angry as he listens to the intruders, who talk freely because they don't realize he understands English—just as, years later, the hospital staff will speak freely thinking he is deaf. The Chief begins correcting the visitors' mistaken notions about Indian houses, but they pay no attention.

And now, perhaps for the first time in his life, fear and anger cause the Chief to have one of his hallucinations. He sees the sun become so bright it reveals the strangers to be machines that ignore words (like his) that don't fit their preconceived ideas.

The squawk of a guinea hen interrupts the hallucination. The two men decide to talk with the Chief's father, but the woman tells them not to. She has another plan. Here is another example of the evil power of matriarchy: the whitehaired lady reminds Chief Bromden of Nurse Ratched, and she acts much as Nurse Ratched does, with a sly knowledge of people's weak points. She realizes that the government will be able to defeat the Chief's father through his mother (the white woman whom we've already been told made the Chief's father small).

The visitors leave. As a final reminder of their ignorance, they call the tribe by the wrong name. (Navajos of course live in the Southwest, hundreds of miles from the Columbia River.)

The Chief is amazed he can remember so much with such clarity. In the first scene, we recall, the fear of the present seeped through to destroy his memories of the past; that hasn't happened here. Something about McMurphy and the idea of a fishing trip has cleared his mind. But the Chief's thoughts are interrupted by an aide cleaning up the gum Chief Bromden has for years stuck under his bed. In the neighboring bunk, McMurphy is angry at the disturbance of his sleep—why couldn't the aide do this work earlier? But then he finds the collected gum amusing.

McMurphy knows the Chief isn't deaf, but this is only the second time he's shown his awareness of that fact. Now he starts to sing to the Chief a popular song, "Does Your Chewing Gum Lose Its Flavor On the Bedpost Overnight?" The Chief, though desperately wanting to laugh, is afraid to reveal his secret. But when McMurphy offers him a stick of gum he says "Thank you"—the first words he has spoken out loud in half a lifetime.

The Chief is out of practice at laughing and at talking, but McMurphy reassures him that he has all night to practice if he wants. The Chief remains silent, though—what he wants to say is something that would show his affection for McMurphy, but he is afraid it would sound odd. So he listens as McMurphy tells him about his own childhood experiences of staying silent while adults paid no attention to him, then getting his revenge. He asks if the Chief is playing the same game.

No, the Chief answers. He is too scared, too small. McMurphy objects that the Chief stands a head taller than any man in the ward. But we understand that the Chief's view of height and size has nothing to do with physical stature and everything to do with psychological strength. His father, so tall he was known as the Pine-That-Stands-Tallest-on-the-Mountain, was made small by his mother. His mother stood only five-foot-nine, but she was a giant.

The Chief says that it wasn't only his mother who made his father small; it was the forces that make up what he calls the Combine. He explains to McMurphy the Combine's workings—how it destroyed the Indian village and waterfall for a dam, how it gave his father money but stole his self-respect. The Chief warns that McMurphy may suffer the same fate: the Combine will install machines to destroy him, just as it destroyed his father by reducing him to a pathetic drunk. The Chief admits that he's been "talking crazy," and McMurphy agrees that he has—but then adds that the Chief's "craziness" makes a certain sense. The Chief is so happy that someone has broken down the wall of fear that isolated him he wants to touch McMurphy, not out of sexual desire (though he briefly fears that is the case) but out of gratitude and love.

McMurphy asks the Chief if he wants to join the fishing trip, trying to heighten the Chief's interest by admitting the "aunts" from Portland are in fact prostitutes. When the Chief confesses that he has no money, McMurphy works out a deal that recalls his failed effort to lift the control panel in scene eleven, Part One, and that foreshadows the end of the book. McMurphy will pay for the Chief's trip, and he promises to make the Chief as big as he once was (which of course means giving the Chief back his self-respect). In return the Chief has to promise to lift the control panel. McMurphy plans to win bets on the stunt.

McMurphy describes the wonderful life the Chief will lead once he regains his size. This is McMurphy's Western, tall tale humor; he could be describing a modern Paul Bunyan: "Well well well, what giant's this *here*, takin' ten feet at a step and duckin' for telephone wires?" Women will pant after the Chief and men will be terrified. McMurphy's talk is convincing. As he leaves to add the Chief's name to the trip list, he lifts up the Chief's bedsheet. Bromden's erection is a sign of his recovery, his re-entry into the world of health and strength.

SCENE 2

This long scene depicts McMurphy's finest hour, an escape from the hospital into the outside world.

On the morning of the trip, the Chief is so excited (apparently as much by the chance to be with two prostitutes from Portland as by the fishing) he awakens even earlier than usual. The aides can't believe his name has been added to the list. He can't write, he can't even read, they laugh, and the newly confident Chief is so angry he walks away when they stick a broom at him as a reminder that he should resume his menial life as a floor-sweeper. The Chief is scared this small act of rebellion will be punished, but thanks to the ruckus McMurphy is making, the aides don't follow him into the day room.

McMurphy is acting as if he were the greatest sailor of all time. While he jokes with the Acutes, the Chronics look at the Chief with envy that he is healthy enough to join the trip and they are not. McMurphy still needs to book another passenger, but it seems that the Nurse has been so successful in convincing the patients of the trip's dangers he won't be able to find anyone. Then George Sorenson, the obsessively clean man who wouldn't even shake McMurphy's hand when he arrived, walks up and gives McMurphy pointers on catching fish; it turns out that George was a commercial fisherman for 25 years. McMurphy grabs at this chance to get an expert passenger. He needs someone like George, he pleads, admitting that he is far from the expert sailor he's been claiming to be. When George balks, too afraid of germs to join the trip, McMurphy tries to appeal to the fisherman's vanity, implying that his real fear is not of germs but of the stories the Nurse has spread about the dangerous ocean. Now George has his own small rebellion: he'll show the Nurse and everyone else that he is not frightened of the sea. He doesn't have $10, but McMurphy lets him join the trip for $5. (Here, as with his offer to the Chief, we see that McMurphy remains enough of a con artist that his generosity is never completely pure. This weakness for the quick buck will be used against him later.)

Only one of the prostitutes shows up, and she is younger, prettier, and more innocent-looking than anyone had expected. Indeed, Candy Starr becomes one of the few entirely sympathetic women characters in the book. Her appearance causes a stir among patients and staff; to the Chief, it's as if the hospital machinery falls apart at the sight of her. The men's stares make Candy nervous, but Billy Bibbit breaks the ice with a wolf whistle, the sort of appreciation she is used to.

Nurse Ratched makes a last attempt to spoil the day by saying that because McMurphy has only one car, half the patients will have to stay behind. Perhaps the entire trip may have to be cancelled. When McMurphy protests that he'll lose money, the Nurse maneuvers him into revealing that he hopes to make a small profit on the expedition. She wants the other patients to see him as a dishonest trickster. "As I think about it now, you've had more than your share of victories," she says—and she is not talking just about money.

But Candy's beauty saves the day, making the doctor susceptible to McMurphy's cajoling to join the trip and take a hospital car. The group leaves. Ellis, who stands in his usual, crucified position against the wall, says farewell using Christ's words to Peter—be a fisher of men. Billy, acting the way McMurphy himself might, turns the farewell into a risque joke about Candy. Like the Chief, he's gaining sexual self-confidence.

Outside! For the first time in the book the Chief has escaped beyond the walls of the hospital. You'll notice that even his descriptions are clearer now—when he comments that "It looked at first like the leaves were hitting the fence and turning into birds and flying away," his use of the words "at first," and "like" turn what could be one of his hallucinations into a rational simile.

But the patients are unsettled by their freedom. They've exposed themselves to the world the Nurse has warned them repeatedly they can't survive. Even Dr. Spivey is nervous. When the two cars pull up to a gas station, the attendant isn't fooled by the doctor's feeble lie that his passengers are not hospital patients but a work crew, and he is ready to cheat them. McMurphy informs the attendant that the passengers are indeed mental patients, and especially dangerous ones at that. The attendant, frightened, backs down, and the other patients follow McMurphy's example.

"He'd shown us what a little bravado and courage could accomplish, and we thought he'd taught us how to use it."

The lesson hasn't fully sunk in yet; the patients are far from being completely healed. No one will laugh, the Chief says, and McMurphy "knew you can't really be strong until you can see a funny side to things." But the Chief wonders if McMurphy is able to see the damage that has been done to the patients, the reasons why they are unable to laugh: if McMurphy can in fact see the Combine.

NOTE: The Combine   Here we see evidence that the Combine is busy at work on the outside as well as inside the hospital. The wild West that was the Chief's home has been defiled by "five thousand houses punched out identical by a machine"; commuter trains deposit businessmen in "mirrored suits and machined hats, laying them like a hatch of identical insects." (One of those businessmen could well be the lobotomized Mr. Taber.) There is no room for anyone different; the different will only suffer, like the one kid the Chief imagines playing crack the whip, always at the end of the line, always the one to fly off and get hurt. This pattern will repeat itself for the rest of the kid's life, as he becomes someone like Harding, or Billy, or the Chief himself.

McMurphy and his 12 followers (note that their number is the same as the number of Christ's disciples: an early likening of McMurphy to Christ) reach the ocean. But the captain and crew of the boat McMurphy has chartered give them trouble: McMurphy can't sail without papers authorizing the trip, the captain announces; the crew makes dirty comments about Candy. Brave with each other in the car, the Chief and the rest of the patients are again afraid when presented with a real threat, and their fear shames them.

But McMurphy fools everyone, taking the patients out on the boat without permission or captain or crew. Out on the ocean, as far from the hospital and Nurse Ratched as they can be, the patients feel a sense of release. McMurphy gives Billy a chance to be alone with Candy, and when Billy refuses, goes below deck with the girl himself. Meanwhile, the other patients are learning to fish under the instruction of George Sorenson, the ex-fishing boat captain who has taken the helm just as he did in the old days. A braver captain than those of the other sportsfishing boats, George doesn't hug the shore but heads out into the open ocean.

The patients are excited. Billy wins the pool for catching the first fish, though it's clear that despite his victory, he'd rather be with Candy. George steers the boat into a school of salmon, the fish begin to bite, and the boat goes wild. No one knows what to do; even Dr. Spivey is calling on McMurphy for help. But McMurphy only laughs. The patients must learn to solve this crisis—and by implication, all the crises of their lives—for themselves, and they do. Harding helps the Chief land his fish.

Candy, who has lost her T-shirt during her time below deck with McMurphy, takes a pole. Billy helps her, at last getting his chance to be near the lovely girl. In the chaos of shouts, flopping salmon, bending fishing poles, George stalls the boat. But McMurphy continues to laugh, because, the Chief says, "he knows you have to laugh at the things that hurt you just to keep yourself in balance, just to keep the world from running you plumb crazy. He knows there's a painful side . . . but he won't let the pain blot out the humor no more'n he'll let the humor blot out the pain."

This is the secret to sanity, to survival. This is the lesson McMurphy has been teaching throughout the book. And now, at last, the patients have learned it, because they, too, are laughing. The Chief has gone them one step further—his description of his feelings reminds us of his description of McMurphy's voice at the start of the book. He's like a bird, flying free above the world.

The doctor, who in his way is as much a victim of Nurse Ratched as are his patients, enjoys his moment of triumph as he lands an enormous salmon. The boat struggles through the high waves the Nurse has warned about, but safely, with Billy getting a chance to be Candy's hero by giving up his life jacket to her. During the rough ride into the harbor, George stands at the helm, unmoving as the mast. He's regained something of his old strength on the trip.

At the dock, the Combine—in the forms of the captain and the local police—are ready to attack, but the doctor (now braver and cagier himself) warns that he will get the captain in trouble over the shortage of life jackets. McMurphy and the captain engage in a brief scuffle, then make peace over beers. The crew that had been rude when the patients left is polite now that they have proved themselves on the ocean, and is full of admiration for George's skill as a sailor. Even George's obsession with cleanliness for once makes humorous sense: to a suggestion that he enter politics he answers he won't because it's "too dirty."

They return to the hospital late. Billy and Candy arrange a date for two in the morning the next Saturday. The patients enter the ward as heroes, but there's an ominous note when one of those who remained

points out how tired McMurphy seems. Harding jok-
ingly claims that McMurphy tired himself out making
love, but the Chief suspects something more serious
is wrong. He remembers the drive back from the
ocean.

They drove through the town where McMurphy
spent his youth. His old house is run-down now, and
his parents are dead. "A good home," he says nostal-
gically. Then, perhaps a little unbelievably, he spots a
rag caught in a tree: put there, he says, by the first girl
he made love to, when he was only ten years old.

NOTE: The Use of Rhyme　　You should note that
the description of this girl, and all of this description of
McMurphy's return to his hometown, is written in
rhyme: "The first girl ever drug me to bed/ Wore that
very same dress./I was about ten and she was probably less/ And at the time a lay seemed like such a big
deal/ I asked her if didn't she think, *feel*/ We ought to
announce it some way?/ Like say, tell our folks, 'Mom/
Judy and me got engaged today." The rhyme empha-
sizes the poetry of McMurphy's memories, memories
which are to him as precious as the Chief's recollections of his Indian village—and as distant from the
grim world of the hospital to which he must now
return.

The little girl teaches McMurphy not just about sex,
but about the occasional rightness of violating the
rules: she knows they don't have to get married just
because they've made love. McMurphy seems full of
his usual bravado as he recalls her. But the tail lights
from a passing car expose his face, and the Chief sees
that McMurphy is in fact very weary. His rough life
has brought him to a prison from which there may be
no escape. Yet it's a measure of his generosity that

despite his weariness, he continues to play the part the patients have come to expect him to play: McMurphy the rogue, the fighter for a freedom that could, perhaps, be theirs.

PART IV

Part IV consists of four scenes.

SCENE 1

We've seen Nurse Ratched plotting against McMurphy; now she makes her first move, trying to undermine the patients' respect for him. Why did McMurphy "spend so much time and energy organizing fishing trips to the coast and arranging Bingo parties and coaching basketball teams? What pushed him to keep up a full head of steam when everybody else on the ward had always been content to drift along playing pinochle and reading last year's magazines?" The Nurse's insinuations are not impossible ones. In fact, she is taking a view that almost all of us have taken in our more cynical moments. Is there such a thing as true generosity? Aren't most people watching out for themselves most of the time? Why should McMurphy be any different?

What's more, McMurphy has left himself vulnerable to her attack. For the fact is he isn't a saint. He's a gambler who likes to win. As a result, the patients are not unwilling to believe the Nurse's rumors. They, too, find it hard to believe that anyone would perform so many acts of kindness without expecting something for himself.

At the group meeting, McMurphy is at first able to fight back, but when he leaves to take a phone call (presumably from Candy), Nurse Ratched can resume her attack without opposition. She's sly about this, as she always is, leading the patients until they say the things about McMurphy she wants them to say: that because McMurphy is not perfect, he must be completely bad, a con artist whose sole reason for being in the hospital is to separate the patients from their money. Billy tries to defend the man who arranged his date with Candy and who has spent hours teaching him to dance, but the Nurse is too clever for him: she insists that she is "not criticizing this activity as such." It's enough that she has planted doubts about McMurphy in everyone's minds. And she drops her attack before McMurphy returns from the phone, so he will remain ignorant of the damage she has done him.

The patients themselves begin spreading similar rumors. Harding tries to defend McMurphy, but his defense is as damaging as the Nurse's attacks: he agrees that McMurphy has had selfish reasons for everything he did, but says that the patients should admire, not condemn, his skill as a con man. Billy still believes in his dancing teacher's good intentions, but when McMurphy informs him that he'll need to pay for Candy's trip from Portland (and that some of the money will go into McMurphy's pocket), he is forced to agree that perhaps the Nurse is correct.

As for the Chief, he still clings to his own belief— "how McMurphy was a giant come out of the sky to save us from the Combine that was networking the land with copper wire and crystal, how he was too big to be bothered with something as measly as money." But he, too, sees evidence otherwise. McMurphy forces him to fulfill his part of the bargain about the fishing trip. The Chief will have to lift the tub room control panel so McMurphy can win his bets. But the other patients, and now even the Chief, see this as a final confirmation that McMurphy is the selfish man

Nurse Ratched claimed he was. McMurphy is puzzled at the Chief's disappointment. Why should anyone object to a man winning some money? He is only now beginning to realize that he has set himself up as an example to the rest of the ward, and that with this role come a number of responsibilities.

The patients are ordered into the shower, supposedly to clean them of vermin acquired on the fishing trip (as if the trip had been such a filthy experience), but actually as punishment for rebelling against the Nurse. Despite their current disillusionment with McMurphy, the patients have changed since his arrival. They aren't as docile as they once would have been, and this makes the aides angry. When the aides reach George, the cleanliness-obsessed fisherman, they insist on giving him an enema with the foul soap, although they know how this will disturb him.

As the aides humiliate George, McMurphy sees that the patients need a hero, and that he is the only possible candidate. He comes to the fisherman's rescue. A brutal fight begins. And then the Chief shows some of the courage McMurphy has already demonstrated. Realizing that McMurphy has been forced to fight George's, and the other patients', battles for them, the Chief decides he must fight, too, "not worrying about anything else for once but the thing that needed to be done and the doing of it." The Chief and McMurphy manage to knock two of the aides unconscious, but they are finally subdued and taken to the Disturbed Ward.

SCENE 2

We're in the Disturbed Ward, where patients pace endlessly and unpleasant smells of burning hang in the air. The fear is enough to make Chief Bromden suffer from the hallucination that one of the Disturbed patients is "dangling from a wire screwed in between his shoulder blades." The patient says, "I wash my hands of the whole deal," his words echoing Pontius Pilate's actions before ordering Christ's crucifixion. (We'll see many more references to Christ shortly.)

McMurphy is in pain from the fight, but he tries to act like his old, bragging self, and the Chief, also in pain, follows his example. For the first time we meet a sympathetic member of the hospital staff, a kindly Japanese-American nurse who explains that not all of the wards in the hospital are as bad as Nurse Ratched's. She suggests that the Nurse's thwarted sexuality is to blame: all unmarried nurses, she says, should quit after they reach 35. Interestingly, McMurphy, who might be expected to agree, replies that the problem isn't that simple—the fault may lie in the fact that Nurse Ratched is an Army Nurse. (It's easy to see the Army as being another arm of the Combine.) Despite the nurse's kindness, she says she is powerless to keep the Chief and McMurphy in the safety of her ward.

The Chief knows what is about to happen to them, and he sleeps restlessly, plagued by nightmares and the voice of the disturbed patient repeating Pilate's words.

The next morning Nurse Ratched and her aides appear, anxious for revenge. Unless McMurphy and the Chief apologize for their fight, they will receive electro-shock therapy. She claims that during a group meeting the very patients McMurphy was fighting for agreed such treatment was necessary. But McMurphy refuses to admit he was wrong. He compares the Nurse's tactics to the ones he experienced in a Chinese prisoner of war camp in the Korean War.

McMurphy and the Chief are taken to the Main Building, which holds the Shock Shop. On the walk there, the Chief looks across the yard and is reminded of the dog he watched from his window weeks before. You can almost see the Chief wondering: Did the dog survive its meeting with the Combine? Will he and McMurphy survive their similar meeting?

When they reach the Shock Shop, other patients are finishing their treatments. One is singing a hymn; another, the ex-football player who lifeguards at the pool, is shouting, "Guts ball! Guts ball!" as he encourages his nonexistent team to play as hard as they can. (Guts, you may remember from Scene 7, Part II, is what Billy Bibbit said he and the other patients lacked.) Frightened, the Chief thinks, "Air Raid," the wartime danger he could escape only by hiding in the fog. As McMurphy leaves for his first treatment, he winks and attempts to tell the Chief something.

NOTE: McMurphy as Christ   Throughout the book we've seen that electro-shock therapy has been used as a symbol of Christ's crucifixion. Ellis, a victim of the treatment, stands perpetually crucified against the Ward's walls; Harding's description of the procedure mentioned its cross-shaped table and electric crown of thorns. As McMurphy approached this punishment, we heard references to Pontius Pilate and a hymn: "It's my cross, thank you Lord, it's all I got, thank you Lord." Now, strapped to the table, McMurphy speaks partly in biblical terms, telling the attendant, "Annointest my head with conductant. Do I get a crown of thorns?" And many readers and critics have asked in what way he is supposed to resemble Christ.

There's no doubt that the book draws many parallels between the two, not just in its mention of electro shock therapy but elsewhere—as in the number of men (twelve) McMurphy leads to the ocean. But at the same time you may remember those "Moby Dick" undershorts and wonder how seriously you should take any symbol in this book. After all, McMurphy is a drinker, a fighter, a gambler, a womanizer—not a saint. He didn't enter the hospital to save souls but to find an easy life. Even now his Christlike words are mixed with radio jingles for hair tonic.

Still, here he is on a cross-shaped table with an electric crown of thorns. Like Christ, he has spread a gospel of light and life in a world of darkness and death, and, after fighting for the salvation of others, is about to be sacrificed.

Now it's the Chief's turn for treatment. As the electricity passes through his head, it brings forth a stream of thoughts about his past—first an air raid in World War II, then a boyhood hunting trip with his father. He feels ants crawling around him and remembers that once his father tricked him into eating some.

We see more of the relationship between the Chief's father and mother. A white woman, she represents the power of the matriarchy, of whites over Indians, of the modern over the old—in short, of the Combine. She is the woman the visitors in Part Three, Scene One, say they will deal with to acquire the Indian village for the government dam. By forcing her husband to agree to this deal, and by forcing him to take on her own white last name (instead of her using his Indian name), she has made the Chief's father "small." Her complete victory is signalled when the

Chief's father says of his new name, "makes gettin'
that Social Security card a lot easier." Thanks to his
wife, the Chief's father has lost both his livelihood and
his identity, and is reduced to charity.

NOTE: The Book's Title   As the Chief recalls a
rhyming game, we see both an explanation of the
book's title, and, in miniature, reminders to many of
the book's themes. The game is "Tingle Tingle Tangle
Toes," which he played with his grandmother.

> Tingle tingle tangle toes
> She's a good fisherman, catches hens
> Puts 'em inna pens.
> Wire blier limber lock
> Three geese inna flock
> One flew east, one flew west
> One flew over the cuckoo's nest
> O-U-T spells out
> Goose sweeps down and plucks you out.

A child again, the Chief says that he doesn't like
Mrs. Tingle Tangle toes, but that he does like his
grandma and the goose. Why? Mrs. Tangle Toes is
one of the Combine, imprisoning fish the way Nurse
Ratched imprisons her patients. As for the geese,
we've seen that throughout the book they are symbols of freedom. Now in this rhyme one of them is
flying over a cuckoo's nest—and cuckoo, of course, is
familiar slang for a crazy person, "cuckoo's nest" a
likely term for a mental hospital. Is Bull Goose Looney
McMurphy the swooping goose in the rhyme? And is
the Chief the one the goose plucks out? Perhaps—but
nothing is certain yet. For the rhyme is just a child's
game; the woman who taught it to the Chief is dead

ignored by whites and Indians alike. And the series of images that follow the rhyme are bleak indeed.

The Chief thinks of Joey Fish In a Barrel, who, like the Chief's father, saw his tribal life destroyed and has found no replacement for it: he received money for his land to buy cars he doesn't know how to drive. The Chief thinks of a crap game. He is the dice, and he is loaded against McMurphy—he and the other patients are destroying McMurphy by encouraging him to sacrifice himself for their benefit.

He wonders what McMurphy said just before he was taken into the Shock Shop. Again he remembers his Indian boyhood, when he was a good student but stripped of confidence—for what can even an educated Indian become except a rug weaver or a drunk? We see him working at a gas station where a customer can't believe he speaks English. He remembers his grandma's funeral; objecting to the white ceremony, his father and his uncle dig up the body to hang it from a tree in a traditional Indian custom. The act sent them to jail.

Now, however, as the treatment comes to a close, the Chief begins to feel better. The images that pass through his mind are more peaceful. Even after death, his grandma is chanting her rhyme. The loaded dice are at rest. And the Chief is able to remember what McMurphy said: "Guts ball." McMurphy has made the Chief big enough to play guts ball; the Chief is now fighting back on his own. As he awakes from the treatment, we're reminded of the book's opening as he says, "They're out there." But the Chief is a different man now. The fog is coming, but, he says, "I won't slip off and hide in it. No . . . never again."

"I saw an aide coming up the hall with a tray for me and knew this time I had them beat."

SCENE 3

The Chief has scored his victory. Before, it might have taken him two weeks to escape the fog brought on by the electroshock therapy. Now it takes only a day. And he's free of the fog for good.

McMurphy, however, isn't so lucky. Because he refuses to give in to Nurse Ratched, he's subjected to more shock treatments. He fights back, pretends he's the same old McMurphy, bragging, pinching the Nurse, insisting that the treatments have caused him no trouble. But the Chief sees the truth in McMurphy's tired face: the Combine is wearing him down.

The Chief leaves the Disturbed Ward and returns downstairs without being able to say goodbye to McMurphy. Harding and the others treat the Chief with the awe they once reserved for the new patient, not even thinking the Chief's sudden burst into speech unusual because they're too busy trying to get information about his friend.

During the group meeting the next day the patients laugh at Nurse Ratched's failure. (But it's an ominous sign when she says that because McMurphy isn't responding to EST, something else—meaning lobotomy—may eventually be tried.) McMurphy is becoming a legend, and Nurse Ratched knows she must prevent that. She plans to bring McMurphy back to the ward, while continuing to inflict shock treatments on him in hopes he'll grow so weak the patients will lose their respect for him.

The Chief and the other patients realize they'll have to arrange for McMurphy's immediate escape. When he returns, seemingly the same rowdy, disruptive man he was before, they tell him their plans. But he objects—tonight is the night his friend Candy is to have her date with Billy Bibbit. He agrees to escape at the end of the evening.

During another group meeting, Nurse Ratched repeats her belief that McMurphy may require stronger treatment. Thinking she means more EST, McMurphy pretends enthusiasm for the idea. When he discovers that she is in fact suggesting a lobotomy, he turns even that suggestion into a joke, implying that she means at last to castrate him.

NOTE: On Sexual Maturity   As the hour of Billy's date with Candy approaches, we're reminded again of the link between freely expressed sexuality and sanity. As with Harding's, Billy's problems are in large part sexual. Throughout the book we've seen him as intelligent, sensitive, but painfully shy—still boyish, even though is over 30. Another of the oppressive, destructive mothers in the book, Mrs. Bibbit has prevented her son from reaching sexual maturity, just as her friend Nurse Ratched has prevented him and the other patients from gaining the maturity that would free them from the hospital. For McMurphy and for Kesey, Billy's imminent loss of virginity is a giant first step towards joining the world of free and functioning men.

Midnight. Most of the patients are still awake, awaiting Candy's arrival. McMurphy asks Mr. Turkle, one of the more sympathetic of the aides, to unlock the Seclusion room for Billy's and Candy's use. As payment, Turkle demands not just liquor but time with Candy himself. Billy, ever-innocent, is angry at this implied denial of Candy's virtue, but McMurphy tells him not to worry—by the time Billy's date arrives, Turkle will be too drunk to think about women.

Turkle and McMurphy smoke marijuana while waiting for Candy. When they think to turn on the ward lights, she finally appears. McMurphy misquotes Byron (the real poem reads "She walks in beauty, like the night"), and drags the nervous Billy to meet her.

Candy is already drunk, and she's brought along an equally drunken friend, Sandy, the girl who was supposed to go on the fishing trip but who got married instead. After an extremely brief marriage, she's back. Like Candy, she seems fun-loving and, in her own way, innocent.

The patients are amazed by the two women. The well-read Harding compares them to characters in novels by Thorne Smith, a popular writer of the 1920s and 30s. The noise of an approaching supervisor scares everyone into the latrine. The supervisor questions Turkle, who can't explain why all the lights in the ward are lit except for the one in the room in which he's working. Harding saves the situation by concocting an absurd story about his need to go to the bathroom in the dark: at last he is combining his intelligence with some courage.

The patients begin to get drunk. Turkle allows them to break into the room where drugs and hospital records are kept, and the patients examine the information the staff has collected on them. Candy is amazed by Billy's file—he doesn't seem as crazy as the hospital reports him to be. Rules are being violated right and left. As Sandy and the epileptic Sefelt make love, he suffers one of his seizures—but the girl seems more impressed than upset.

Harding makes a speech that he intends to be humorous, but which is, at least for some members of the ward, sadly true. "It is our last fling," he announces. "We are henceforth doomed." Despite his words, the party continues. Billy and Candy disappear into the Seclusion room. The Chief wonders if the evening's antics have shown that the Combine isn't really all-powerful. He feels so good about this hope that he hoists McMurphy and Sandy as easily as if they were kids—an indication that he's regained his true size.

The night is almost over, and some of the patients are going to bed. Harding, sensible even when drunk, suggests a plan: they should tie up Turkle, making it seem that McMurphy went on the rampage. Once McMurphy escapes, Harding says, it will be unlikely that anyone will search for him.

McMurphy agrees. But he's tired and wants to know why the others won't make the escape with him. They're still not ready, Harding says. This answer seems to frighten McMurphy. He asks, "Then what makes you think I am?"

Harding tries to answer. Like the Chief, Harding has gained strength, thanks to the new patient's example. He no longer uses his intelligence as a means of fooling himself or belittling others. Even the hands that he found so embarrassing now show his health; the Chief says that they "shaped what he said," honestly, without shame. Harding admits that he doesn't really know why he and the other patients were so weak. In his case, it may have been that society's disapproval of his homosexuality sent him to the hospital. He knows, however, that this isn't McMurphy's problem. "It's us," he says. Like the Chief, Harding realizes that the patient's need for McMurphy has brought McMurphy to sacrifice himself.

McMurphy plans to leave at 6 a.m., but first he wants to get some sleep. As he says goodbye, Harding compares him to the Lone Ranger, riding away from the people he's saved. McMurphy tells Harding he is now the ward's new Bull Goose Looney, and we realize that Harding is strong enough to deserve the title he couldn't win at the book's start. As for the Chief, McMurphy doesn't know what title he can claim—a hint, perhaps, that the Chief has not yet found out who he should be, or perhaps that he is so much larger than McMurphy that McMurphy can't see him clearly.

The plan is put into action. Turkle is tied up. McMurphy and Sandy go to bed, "more like two tired kids than a grown woman and man in bed together to make love." The Chief's description of the pair is reminiscent of McMurphy's own description of his first girlfriend, Judy, and it's a reminder of McMurphy's childlike vulnerability at this point in the novel. He is weakened and tired: he and Sandy sleep too long and are caught by aides in the morning.

SCENE 4

The final scene in the book begins with the Chief announcing that McMurphy's escape would have been doomed even if he had left the hospital at 6 as planned. Somehow he would have heard what Nurse Ratched did to Billy, and he would have been forced to return for a final showdown with her.

The hospital has never seen anything like this morning. At first the patients stand solemn and still as the evidence of their disobedience is gathered, but soon each new reminder of last night's party—cough syrup bottles, wheelchairs—amuses them as much as it angers the Nurse.

Turkle lets Sandy escape, and Harding urges McMurphy to follow her. But McMurphy, who looks "sick and terrifically tired," refuses. One of the aides notices that Billy Bibbit is missing, but no one will admit they know where he is. This refusal of her patients to spill their secrets further enrages Nurse Ratched.

Billy and Candy are discovered in the Seclusion room. Sleepy, still a little drunk, they ignore the Nurse's outrage at first. Billy is pleased that he's gained his manhood, but the Nurse will not let him remain a man. She uses all of her powers to reduce him once more to a disobedient child. She will have to tell Mrs. Bibbit what Billy did, she warns, and Mrs. Bibbit will be very disappointed. The tactic works. Billy begs the Nurse not to tell, blames his situation on Candy, on McMurphy, even on Harding. Seconds before, he could speak without stuttering: now he is again a stuttering, weak-willed child. Nurse Ratched sends him into the doctor's office.

The Chief looks at McMurphy and sees that, although he is tired, he is just "resting a second before he came out for the next round" of the fight. The Combine never lets up; all you can do is keep fighting until you're worn down, then send someone else to fight in your place. The doctor goes into his office and discovers that Billy has killed himself by cutting his throat. The Nurse immediately blames McMurphy for this death, just as she blamed him for Cheswick's.

The Chief knows that the final battle is about to begin. He would like to prevent it but realizes that he can't. He and the other patients are the people who are making McMurphy fight the Nurse; during his last weeks of shock therapy, their need for him has given him his only reason to go on living.

Now, for a few minutes, McMurphy is his old self, a movie cowboy, his cap a Stetson, his bare feet jangling on the floor tiles as if they were spurred. Once again he breaks the glass of Nurse Ratched's office. This time, however, he doesn't stop with that: he attacks her, too. Up to a point, the attack succeeds. The Nurse's smiling, doll-like face can never hold the power it once held, now that it has shown such terror; the breasts visible under the ripped uniform reveal what the Nurse has so long tried to deny—that she, too, is a human being, not a sexless, perfectly tuned machine.

But McMurphy's victory is brief. Battered by supervisors, he falls unconscious, crying like a cornered, dying animal.

The Chief tells us that he remained in the hospital for a few weeks more, simply to see what would happen to the Ward. Many changes do occur. Though McMurphy has lost the war for himself, he has won it for others. Patients are feeling brave enough to sign themselves out of the hospital, or at least out of Nurse Ratched's ward. The doctor, too, shows uncharacteristic courage: when pressured to resign, he announces the hospital will have to fire him. Harding takes on McMurphy's old role as card sharp and Bull Goose Looney.

Nurse Ratched returns changed, too. Her new uniform can't disguise the fact that she is a woman. Unable to talk since the attack, she communicates by writing, but her written words can't inspire the fear her voice did. She is powerless against McMurphy's growing legend. More patients, Harding among them, leave the hospital; of the fishing crew, McMurphy's disciples, only Martini, Scanlon, and the Chief remain.

Then McMurphy returns. Sadly, he, too, is a different man. Lobotomized, he has become one of the vegetables. Scanlon and Martini refuse to believe that this white-faced shell is the same person who led so many brave revolts, but the Chief knows the truth. He knows it would be a crime if the Nurse were able to make McMurphy into another Mr. Taber, a symbol of her power, a warning not to fight.

That night the Chief moves to McMurphy's bed and stands over him, watching his friend's "open and undreaming" eyes. He smothers McMurphy with a pillow. After McMurphy's breathing halts, the Chief notices that his eyes have not changed at all. In effect, he was dead before, destroyed by the Nurse, by the Combine.

Scanlon has watched what the Chief has done. He warns that even though the Nurse won't be able to prove the Chief smothered McMurphy—deaths after lobotomies are common—she will realize he is responsible, and will want to take revenge. The Chief must escape.

"How?" Chief Bromden asks.

Scanlon answers that McMurphy has shown him how. The Chief thinks a few minutes before making up his mind. He dresses and tries to put on McMurphy's old cap. But it is too small for him. Thanks to McMurphy, the Chief has regained his true size—and it is greater than McMurphy's.

The Chief goes into the tub room and walks to the control panel that, weeks before, McMurphy told him he was big enough to lift. McMurphy has kept his promise to the Chief. He was not himself strong enough to lift the panel, nor strong enough to escape.

But his example has given the Chief a new life. The Chief lifts the panel, throws it through the strong-screened window, and "glass splashes out in the moon, like a bright cold water baptizing the sleeping earth"—a symbol of the Chief's rebirth. He escapes, running across the field in the same direction the dog ran and the geese flew, toward freedom.

Freedom is dangerous. Like the dog, the Chief may be heading towards an uncertain and possibly disastrous destination. The man who on page one startled us by saying "They're out there," has finished the story he wants to tell us, but his own story is far from finished. He doesn't know where he'll go. Maybe to Canada, home of the geese, but maybe back to his Indian village. He's heard rumors that members of his tribe are fighting the Combine by building scaffolds on the dam, spearing salmon just as they did in the old days. Perhaps this return to the natural world of his boyhood will finish the cure that McMurphy so nobly began. It will take awhile before the Chief is completely healed: he's been away a long time.

A STEP BEYOND

Tests and Answers

TESTS

Test 1

1. A clever technique employed by Ken Kesey   _____
is
A. the telling of his story through dialogue
B. the selection of symbolic names for each character
C. the use of Chief Bromden as a narrator

2. The opening line of the novel, "They're out   _____
there" displays
A. McMurphy's distinction between Good and Evil
B. the Chief's paranoia
C. Nurse Ratched's vision of the patients as subhumans

3. The name which Bromden assigns to   _____
organized society is the
A. Machine
B. Combine
C. Strait-jacket

4. Nurse Ratched's fog machine is equated   _____
with
A. the Chief's state of confusion
B. McMurphy's ability to cloud the issues
C. Dale Harding's total helplessness

5. The best way to survive in the ward is to   _____
A. flatter Nurse Ratched

    B. conform

    C. pay off the orderlies

6. McMurphy stands out in the ward because   _____
   he
   A. has retained his individuality
   B. entered voluntarily
   C. relishes the challenge of Nurse Ratched

7. The patients see themselves as   _____
   A. rabbits
   B. condemned men
   C. victims of the technological revolution

8. In failing to lift the control panel,   _____
   McMurphy
   A. manages to win the confidence of the
      inmates
   B. demonstrates that he cannot be trusted
   C. smashes the Chief's dream of freedom

9. The first "uprising" of the patients occurs in   _____
   the
   A. protest over the gambling
   B. television incident
   C. initial Group Therapy session

10. Ken Kesey's fondness for symbolism is seen in   _____
    his use of the
      I. dog on the lawn
     II. geese flying south
    III. rat in the trap
    A. I and II only   B. I and III only   C. II and III only

11. In a letter to a friend, Kesey stated that point of view
    "truly is the most important problem in writing."
    Describe the ways in which having *One Flew Over the
    Cuckoo's Nest* written from Chief Bromden's point of
    view influences the novel.

12. Describe the nature of the Combine.

13. Who stands victorious at the novel's end?

Test 2

1. Cheswick commits suicide by   _____
   A. swallowing lye
   B. stuffing a pillow case in his mouth
   C. swimming to the pool's bottom

2. Dale Harding is fenced in by Nurse Ratched   _____
   and
   A. McMurphy
   B. his wife
   C. Electro-Shock therapy

3. The ringing in the Chief's ears stopped   _____
   when
   A. Billy killed himself
   B. Dr. Spivey sided with McMurphy
   C. McMurphy smashed the glass

4. When the Chief said he was reduced in size,   _____
   McMurphy
   A. promised to "blow him back up"
   B. showed him that he was actually 6' 7"
   C. sank to his knees

5. One of the ironies of the book is that   _____
   A. as the others improve, McMurphy
      deteriorates
   B. when the Chief finally speaks it is too
      late
   C. Nurse Ratched actually liked McMurphy

6. Many critics have pointed out Ken Kesey's   _____
   indebtedness to
   A. the Bible

    B. Melville's *Moby-Dick*
    C. Conrad's *Heart of Darkness*

7. In sacrificing himself to free the others, ——— McMurphy
    I. points out the Nurse's moral bankruptcy
    II. becomes Christ-like
    III. inspires the Chief to be "reborn"
    A. I and II only   B. II and III only   C. I, II, and III

8. By playing upon Billy's sense of guilt, Nurse ——— Ratched
    A. sets a powerful example for the ward
    B. is able to free him from McMurphy's influence
    C. pushes him to his suicide

9. In smothering McMurphy, the Chief ———
    A. carries out his promise to his friend
    B. strikes a real blow at the Nurse's power
    C. asserts his own individuality

10. The Chief's escape at the end of the novel ——— stands for
    I. his return to life
    II. McMurphy's "triumph" over Nurse Ratched
    III. the symbolic negligence of those who are in power
    A. I and II only   B. I and III only   C. I, II, and III

11. Discuss McMurphy's development as a character through the course of the novel.

12. Analyze the role of women in *One Flew Over the Cuckoo's Nest*.

13. What are the causes of mental illness in *Cuckoo's Nest*?

ANSWERS

Test 1

1. C   **2.** B   **3.** B   **4.** A   **5.** B   **6.** A

7. A   **8.** A   **9.** B   **10.** A

11. We see almost as soon as we begin reading *Cuckoo's Nest* that Kesey's narrator is incapable of giving us descriptions of events as we might see them. In the Chief's paranoid fantasies, the hospital is an enormous whirring machine, its staff soulless cogs. Occasionally a fog creeps in to obscure everything around him. However, Kesey gives us two hints as to how we should take the Chief's visions, when he has the Chief say: (Scene 1, Part I) "But it's the truth even if it didn't happen;" and (Scene 7, Part I), "But how can a man see such things if they don't exist?" The answer, of course, is that they *do* exist, in a metaphorical sense; the hallucinations are structured to give us an understanding of the hospital we wouldn't get through normal description. We see the truth beneath the surface that a more rational narrator might show us.

Having the story told from the Chief's troubled mind also magnifies the importance of the battle being fought. From the Chief's "shrunken" vantage point, McMurphy and the Nurse are enormous, Super-hero and Super-villain, fighting for the souls of the patients. When at the end of part one McMurphy moves towards the Chief, the rescue attempt is doubly stirring because we've had such a vivid sense of how deadly—yet how strangely alluring—is the fog in which the Chief cowers. And after that rescue we're privileged to see the healing process not only as an outside observer might (as in the Chief's growing defiance of the aides), but from within as well, as his descriptions of the ward become less hallucination-prone and more rational, and the fog disappears never to return.

12. The Combine is Chief Bromden's vision of the forces
    that run the hospital and that seek to run the outside
    world as well. Perhaps because his first encounter with
    it came when it destroyed his Indian village for a hydro-
    electric dam, he tends to see it as an enormous electri-
    fied machine, a machine whose chief cog in the hospital
    is Nurse Ratched. The Combine demands efficiency,
    total cooperation, order; it denies individuality and free-
    dom. The men in Nurse Ratched's ward are there, the
    Chief says, because they have malfunctioned: the
    Acutes may yet be fixed, but the Chronics, like the
    Chief, are useless culls who must be imprisoned "to
    keep them from walking around the streets giving the
    product a bad name."

    Outside, the Combine is scarcely less powerful. Its
    dam destroyed hundreds of centuries of Indian tradi-
    tion; its tethers yank the girl in the cotton mill back to
    her work station; its automobile will probably kill the
    freedom-loving dog the Chief views from his window;
    it has despoiled the landscape with identical houses that
    shelter identical businessmen and their identical fami-
    lies.

    Like almost all of the Chief's hallucinations, this one
    contains considerable truth. As McMurphy tells him,
    "Yeah Chief, you be talking crazy . . . [but] I didn't say it
    didn't make sense." The Combine may not be the enor-
    mous conglemeration of machinery the Chief sees, but
    perhaps it does exist in the forces that demand us to
    work, consume, obey, and be indistinguishable from
    our neighbors. You could argue that this philosophy is a
    limited one: after all, mental patients require some order
    in their lives; the dam that destroyed the village pro-
    vides needed electricity; even insectlike businessmen
    need to live somewhere. But Kesey would certainly dis-
    agree with you.

13. *One Flew Over the Cuckoo's Nest* concludes on a note of apparent triumph, as the Chief hurls the control panel through the ward window, escapes the hospital and begins to hitchhike north. But the triumph may not be complete. Indeed, for most of the book the Chief has been the one to tell us that triumphs over the Combine can never be complete. As he says of its main cog, Nurse Ratched (in Scene 9, Part I): "She'll go on winning, just like the Combine . . . she don't lose on her losses but she wins on ours. To beat her you don't have to whip her two out of three or three out of five, but every time you meet. As soon as you let down your guard, as soon as you lose *once*, she's won for good. And eventually we all got to lose. Nobody can help that." And at the end of the novel, many have lost. Cheswick and Billy are dead, McMurphy is a ruined man saved from becoming another Mr. Taber only when the Chief kills him. Nurse Ratched's power may be reduced, but she is able to return to the ward.

Still, if McMurphy has not been able to escape the Combine, he has given the Chief and other patients the courage and strength to continue. As the Chief says just before McMurphy's final battle with the Nurse, "The thing he was fighting, you couldn't whip it for good. All you could do was keep on whipping it, till you couldn't come out any more and somebody else had to take your place." For now, that somebody else is the Chief. Years before, the Combine destroyed his tribe by destroying the waterfall on which their salmon fishing depended. Now, the Chief tells us, the tribe has returned and is using the Combine's dam to spear fish just as they did in the old days—a small but significant act of rebellion the Chief may join. So long as the Chief and others continue the fight, McMurphy can't be said to have lost.

Test 2

1. C   **2.** B   **3.** C.   **4.** A   **5.** A   **6.** B
7. B   **8.** C   **9.** B   **10.** A

11. McMurphy enters the ward as more a rogue than a hero, despite his humor and obvious courage. The Chief may be speaking at least part of the truth when he says McMurphy has survived because he had "no one to care about, which is what made him free enough to be a good con man." Though he immediately rebels against the Nurse and the hospital, his rebellion is staged primarily for his own benefit—it's McMurphy who wants to brush his teeth, to play cards undisturbed by piped-in music, to watch the World Series on television. But when, scared by the discovery that Nurse Ratched can keep him indefinitely in the hospital, he backs down and a disillusioned follower commits suicide, McMurphy begins to realize that he has become an example of courage to the rest of the patients and that such a role carries with it responsibilities. He doesn't become entirely altruistic all at once—he still forces the Chief to lift the control panel to win bets, for example, and asks Billy for money to bring Candy Starr back down for their date—but in the final scenes it has become clear (at least to the Chief and so to us) that McMurphy is acting the part of hero even at the expense of his own sanity and safety. Indeed, at the end, the hero is the only part of him that remains: the rest of McMurphy has been destroyed by the hospital. The Chief says of his friend's final battle with the Nurse: "It was us that had been making him go on for weeks keeping him standing long after his feet and legs had given out, weeks of making him wink and grin and laugh and go on with his act long after his humor had been parched dry between two electrodes." In this way, out of highly unpromising material, a hero has been made.

12. "We are victims of a matriarchy here, my friend." Harding's explanation of life in the hospital seems to a large extent to be true. While the Combine undoubtedly contains both male and female components, its main representatives in the book do appear to be women. Heading it in the hospital is of course Nurse Ratched, who dominates even men like Dr. Spivey who are nominally her superiors. Her power is expressed in bluntly sexual terms: she is, McMurphy says after his first group meeting, "a ball-cutter." Other such women include Mary Louise Bromden, who forced her husband to give up both his name and his Indian ways; Mrs. Bibbit, who dominated her son at home just as her friend Nurse Ratched dominates him in the hospital; Vera Harding, whose sneering attacks on her husband's effeminacy destroyed his spirit, and minor characters like the birth-marked Nurse Pilbow, so terrified of the sexuality McMurphy represents she becomes a model of pill-spilling hysteria.

Such women gain their power over men in two ways. They oppress men's sexuality. Harding and McMurphy agree that Nurse Ratched's control comes from the fact that men can't be sexually aroused by her; Mrs. Bibbit has prevented Billy from becoming a functioning adult by preventing him from losing his virginity. Just as important, they destroy men's ability to laugh. McMurphy says, "A man go around lettin' a woman whip him down till he can't laugh anymore, and he loses one of the biggest edges he's got on his side. First thing you know he'll begin to think she's tougher than he is. . ."

Opposed to the Nurse and her kind are women like Candy Starr and her friend, Sandy, the Japanese-American nurse, the girl in the cotton mill. These women are, if not sexually free, at least unafraid of their sexuality.

This blaming of the ills of modern society on women,

and the seeming division of women into castrators and good-hearted whores, may have been at least slightly inadvertent on Kesey's part. He does have McMurphy state that ball-cutters can be "young and old, men and women"; the girl in the cotton mill is as much a victim of the Combine as Chief Bromden; McMurphy points out that Dale Harding treats his wife fully as badly as she treats him. In these portions of the book we can see possibilities of sexual equality the rest of *Cuckoo's Nest* seems to deny.

13. The patients in Nurse Ratched's ward have entered the hospital after suffering a variety of failures in the outside world: Harding's bitter marriage, Billy's domination by his mother, the Chief's years of mistreatment as an Indian. And they suffer a variety of symptoms: Billy's stuttering, the Chief's apparent deaf-muteness, Harding's uncontrollable hands.

Yet in Kesey's view—which is that of a novelist, not a psychiatrist—the men are not so much victims of mental illness as of fear instilled in them by society. Unlike McMurphy, they are unable to accept themselves as they are, with all their flaws, all their contradictions, and this makes them easy prey for Nurse Ratched and her allies. As the Chief says when he looks at himself in the mirror, "It don't seem like I ever have been me." Harding puts it even more openly. He came to the hospital, he says, out of "Guilt. Shame. Fear. Self-belittlement. . . . I indulged in certain practices that our society regards as shameful. And I got sick. It wasn't the practices, I don't think, it was the feeling that the great, deadly pointing forefinger of society was pointing at me—and the great voice of millions chanting, 'Shame. Shame. Shame.' "

Only by ignoring that voice, Kesey seems to be saying, can men enjoy the laughter and the free sexuality that is their birthright; only by fighting fear can they remain sane.

Term Paper Ideas

General Topics

1. "You Have to Laugh at the Things That Hurt You:" Laughter in *Cuckoo's Nest*.

2. Sexuality in *Cuckoo's Nest*.

3. Sanity versus insanity in *Cuckoo's Nest*.

4. Nothing to fear but fear itself? Causes of mental illness.

5. The gospel according to McMurphy.

Character Analysis

1. McMurphy as Christ.

2. McMurphy's disciples.

3. Nurse Ratched: character or caricature?

4. In defense of Nurse Ratched.

5. McMurphy As Western hero.

6. The fall of McMurphy, the rise of the Chief.

7. The true hero of *Cuckoo's Nest*: McMurphy or Chief Bromden?

8. McMurphy: con-man to hero.

9. The supporting cast: Billy Bibbit and Dale Harding.

Social Issues

1. The group versus the individual.

2. The ward as microcosm of the outside world.

3. Does the Combine represent reality?

4. Indian life in *Cuckoo's Nest*.

5. The matriarchy: is Kesey unfair to women?
6. *Cuckoo's Nest* and current psychiatric techniques: how accurate a representation?
7. Anti-Establishment politics in *Cuckoo's Nest*.
8. McMurphy and the politics of frontier individualism.

Literary Technique

1. Foreshadowing in *Cuckoo's Nest*.
2. Images of machinery in *Cuckoo's Nest*.
3. "The truth even if it didn't happen:" Chief Bromden's hallucinations.

Poetry and Metaphor in *Cuckoo's Nest*

1. Rhyme and song in *Cuckoo's Nest*.
2. Kesey's use of symbolism.
3. Hands and faces as indications of character.

Comparisons with other works

1. *Cuckoo's Nest* and comic strips.
2. Popular culture in *Cuckoo's Nest*.
3. *Cuckoo's Nest* and *Sometimes a Great Notion*.
4. Billy Bibbit and *Billy Budd*.
5. Kesey and Melville.
6. *Cuckoo's Nest* as novel, "Cuckoo's Nest" as film (or play).

Further Reading

CRITICAL WORKS

Barsness, John A. "Ken Kesey: The Hero in Modern Dress." *Bulletin of the Rocky Mountain Modern Language Association* 23 (1969): 27–33; reprinted in Pratt, pp. 419–28.

Boyers, Robert. "Attitudes toward Sex in American 'High Culture.'" *Annals of the American Academy of Political and*

Social Science 376 (1968): 36–52; part reprinted in Pratt, pp. 535–41.

Kael, Pauline. *When the Lights Go Down.* New York: Holt, Rhinehart and Winston, 1980. Pages 84–90.

Leeds, Barry H. *Ken Kesey.* New York: Ungar, 1981.

Lex et Scientia, 13, nos. 1–2 (1977).

Olderman, Raymond M. *Beyond the Waste land: A Study of the American Novel in the Nineteen-Sixties.* New Haven: Yale University Press, 1972, pp 35–51.

Porter, M. Gilbert. *The Art of Grit: Ken Kesey.* Columbia: University of Missouri Press, 1981.

Pratt, John Clark, ed. *One Flew Over the Cuckoo's Nest: Text and Criticism.* New York: Viking Press, 1973.

Sherwood, Terry G. "*One Flew Over the Cuckoo's Nest* and the Comic Strip." *Critique* 13 (1971): 96–109; reprinted in Pratt, 382–96.

Tanner, Stephen L. *Ken Kesey.* Boston: Twayne Publishers, 1983.

Tanner, Tony. *City of Words: American Fiction 1950–1970.* New York: Harper and Row. 1971.

Waldmeir, Joseph J. "Two Novelists of the Absurd: Heller and Kesey." *Wisconsin Studies in Contemporary Literature* 5 (1964) 192–204; reprinted in Pratt, 401–418.

Wallace, Ronald. *The Last Laugh: Form and Affirmation in the Contemporary American Comic Novel.* Columbia: University of Missouri Press, 1979, pp. 90–115.

Wolfe, Tom. *The Electric Kool-Aid Acid Test.* New York: Farrar, Straus & Giroux, 1968.

AUTHOR'S OTHER WORKS

Sometimes a Great Notion. New York: Viking, 1964.

Kesey's Garage Sale. New York: Viking, 1973

"Abdul and Ebeneezer." *Esquire,* March 1976, pp. 57–58, 146–49.

"The Day After Superman Died." *Esquire*, October 1979, pp. 43–64.

Glossary

Aides   The three black daytime aides—Washington, Williams, and Warren—are examples of the way the Combine turns its victims into the victimizers of others. Undoubtedly, they've suffered racial abuse similar to that which Chief Bromden suffered or worse—in fact, we're told that at age five one of the aides saw his mother raped by a white man. And they continue to suffer under Nurse Ratched, who has instilled in them the same kind of fear she has instilled in her patients

But far from allying themselves with the Nurse's other victims, the aides are anxious to take out their hatred on the one group of people weaker than themselves. They take advantage of every opportunity they get to assault the patients physically, sexually, and psychologically. They demonstrate the power of the Combine at its most brutal. The Nurse is limited in the kinds of punishment she can personally inflict. She can't employ physical force herself and she must disguise her cruelties with smiles and soft words. The aides are under no such restrictions. They are "out there performing her bidding before she even thinks of it."

Acutes   Those patients who, in the staff's opinion, have the potential to be cured. They include Harding, Billy Bibbit, Cheswick, Sefelt and Fredrickson.

Pete Bancini   A Chronic patient, permanently damaged at birth, his cries of "I'm tired" and "it's all a lotta baloney," are the only true words spoken at the Group Meeting.

Mrs. Bibbit   Billy Bibbit's domineering mother, she has kept her son from maturing into manhood, perhaps (her words and wildly dyed hair suggest) because she is afraid of aging herself. A close friend of Nurse Ratched, whom in her desire for control she resembles.

Captain Block The captain of the boat McMurphy charters, he refuses to let the patients go out to sea because they lack proper authorization papers: another example of the Combine's devotion to petty rules.

Mary Louise Bromden The Chief's mother, a white woman who felt she married beneath her by marrying an Indian. Another of the book's domineering women, she forces the Chief's father to take her name and to sell his tribal village to the government for a dam. The Chief blames her for making his father "small."

Cheswick A would-be rebel, he always backed down because he lacked allies. When McMurphy arrives, he gains courage; but when McMurphy begins to obey Nurse Ratched, Cheswick grows so depressed he drowns himself. His death forces McMurphy to confront his responsibilities as a hero-figure to the patients.

Chronics Those patients who in the staff's opinion are incurably mentally ill. They're subdivided into Walkers (Chief Bromden, Ellis, Ruckley, George Sorenson), Wheelers (Colonel Matterson) and Vegetables (Old Blastic).

Combine The Chief's vision of the huge machinelike organization that runs the hospital and seeks to run the entire world. Nurse Ratched is a part of it; so are the government agencies that destroyed the Chief's tribal village. Although a product of the Chief's illness, the Combine represents actual forces at work in the modern world: people and groups who value efficiency over individuality, the mechanical over the natural, and control over freedom.

Disturbed Ward The home for patients more troubled than the men in Nurse Ratched's ward below it, it's run, ironically, by a Japanese-American nurse much more kindly than Nurse Ratched. The Chief and McMurphy stay there on their way to electro shock therapy.

Electro-Shock Therapy A treatment in which electricity is sent through the brain in an effort to calm the patient. Once commonly used, it is now out of favor—except with Nurse Ratched. Numerous references link the treatment to Christ's crucifixion.

Ellis A Chronic patient damaged by an overdose of electro-shock therapy. His spread-armed stance against the wall is one of the devices linking the therapy to the crucifixion, and so linking McMurphy to Christ.

Fredrickson An Acute patient who, like Cheswick, often tries to rebel but always backs down, Fredrickson is so afraid of epileptic seizures he agrees to take his friend Sefelt's dose of anti-seizure drug as well as his own, despite the drug's side-effects.

Grandma The Chief's Indian grandmother, she gives the book its title when she chants her rhyme, Tingle Tingle Tangle Toes, during the recollections brought on by the Chief's electroshock therapy.

Group Meeting A daily meeting at which the patients are expected to discuss their problems with each other and with Nurse Ratched and Dr. Spivey. Nurse Ratched has twisted this potentially useful therapy into another means of maintaining her control over the patients, by leading them to attack one another. McMurphy describes the meetings as "pecking parties."

Vera Harding Dale Harding's wife, she terrifies her husband with her voluptuous figure, her sexual demands, and her attacks on his weakness and effeminacy. In some ways one of the castrating, domineering women of the book, in other ways not—for far from repressing her sexuality, she exaggerates it, and after McMurphy meets her, he suggests that Harding treats her as badly as she does him. When Harding leaves the hospital, he returns to her.

Japanese Nurse This nurse, in charge of the Disturbed Ward, is one of the few fully sympathetic staff members (and women) in the novel. She knows that Nurse Ratched's rule is destructive, but is unable to help the Chief and McMurphy. When Nurse Ratched is hospitalized after McMurphy's attack, she substitutes on the ward and makes long-needed changes.

Lifeguard An ex-football player who still believes he's on a team, the lifeguard meets McMurphy at the pool and informs him that patients don't have fixed sentences in the hospital but can be held at the staff's whim. His cry of "Guts ball" is repeated by McMurphy to the Chief just before they go in for electroshock therapy.

Lobotomy Like electro-shock therapy, a treatment for mental illness once common but now rarely used. The frontal lobe of the brain is removed to make the patient docile, at the expense of his personality.

Martini A patient whose illness makes him see objects—Monopoly pieces, most hilariously—where they don't exist.

Matriarchy A society where power lies entirely in the hands of women. (The word is derived from the Latin for mother.) Dale Harding believes that the patients' plight can be blamed on a matriarchy run by women like Nurse Ratched and his wife, who seek to make men cowardly and impotent. Other women who seem to prove his theory include Mrs. Bibbit and Mary Louise Bromden.

Colonel Matterson This elderly Chronic, an ex-Army officer, speaks in phrases that sound nonsensical but in fact possess poetic, metaphorical truth: "Mexico is . . . the walnut."

Nurse's Station The glassed-in room that holds Nurse Ratched's control panel and is a symbol of her power over the ward. McMurphy's shattering of its window forms the climax of Part Two.

Old Blastic An ancient Chronic, he dies on the night when the Chief, free from sedation, is suffering hallucinations of the hospital as an enormous machine. The Chief imagines that Blastic dies when scalped by the aides.

Old Rawler A patient on the Disturbed Ward, he commits suicide by castrating himself.

Psychosis The mental illness McMurphy is diagnosed as suffering from, victims of psychosis—psychotics—are characterized by a complete disregard of moral and social responsibilities, an inability to think of anything but their own immediate gratification.

Public Relations Man A plump, chatty little man who conducts tours of the hospital for local community groups in order to assure them of the hospital's dedication to its patients' health. His silliness and hypocrisy are signalled in his absurd, almost hysterical laugh, and, in the Chief's nightmare, a vision of him wearing a corset trimmed with male genitals.

Ruckley Like Ellis, a victim of the hospital's therapeutic techniques, Ruckley underwent a lobotomy at a time when the operation had not been perfected. He was left unable to do anything except stare at a blank photograph and shout a single phrase of hatred against his wife.

Scanlon An Acute patient whose fantasies focus on bombs and violence, Scanlon is one of the few to remain in the hospital after McMurphy's lobotomy. In the last scene he warns the Chief of the need to escape, and reminds him that McMurphy has shown him how that escape might be made.

Sefelt An epileptic terrified his antiseizure medicine will make him prematurely old, Sefelt gives his doses to his friend Fredrickson. The damned-if-you-do, damned-if-you-don't plight of the two men forces McMurphy to rethink his own situation.

Shock Shop A nickname for the electro-shock therapy room.

George Sorenson Called Big George for his size, and Rub-a-dub George for his obsession with cleanliness, this ex-fisherman is, like the Chief and Harding, transformed by McMurphy's courage. He pilots the fishing boat expertly after McMurphy convinces him to join the trip; later, in the shower, when the aides abuse him, McMurphy comes to his rescue, starting a fight that sends McMurphy and the Chief to the Shock Shop.

Dr. Spivey Chosen by the Nurse for his timidity (and, it's hinted, for a morphine habit that makes him vulnerable to blackmail), Dr. Spivey is concerned more for his theories and papers than for the welfare of his patients. He begins in the novel completely under the Nurse's control. However, McMurphy infuses him with courage and at the book's end he stands up to the Nurse and to the hospital, refusing to resign.

Candy Starr A prostitute from Portland, Candy is one of the few fully sympathetic female characters in the book. Young and, despite her profession, innocent, she accompanies McMurphy on the fishing trip and later returns to the ward so that Billy may lose his virginity to her—a date that results in Billy's death and in McMurphy's final battle with the Nurse.

Maxwell Wilson Taber Like McMurphy, Mr. Taber was a disruptive influence in Nurse Ratched's ward. She defeats him by forcing him to undergo a lobotomy that reduces him to a productive but characterless member of society—in the Chief's view, just another cog in the Combine.

Tee Ah Millatoona The Chief's father, a Columbia Indian Chief whose name means The-Pine-That-Stands-Tallest-on-the-Mountain. An enormous man able to defeat his enemies by laughing at them (as McMurphy does), Chief Bromden's father was weakened by his wife and by the Combine: his wife forced him to take her white name and sell off his tribal village to the government for a hydro-electric dam; the government (the Combine, in the Chief's view) built the dam that destroyed the village and reduced the Chief's father to an alcoholic charity case. His fate is one of the prime causes of Chief Bromden's illness.

Mr. Turkle A night aide friendlier than his daytime counterparts, Turkle's main vice is drinking. Bribed with liquor, he allows the patients to stage the wild party that forms the book's climax.

The Critics

[McMurphy's] "defeat" along with Kesey's faultless portrayal of institutionalized and aberrant minds, has as much as anything else concealed the heroic fable which is the foundation for this black comedy. But it is not defeat. This hero is too much of an individual, too powerful, actually too successful for that. Though he does not escape, his ally, the Columbia Indian Chief Broom does, and in him the natural man ultimately triumphs. For it is Chief Broom, the Indian pretending dumbness in the face of civilization's blind indifference to him, who rescues McMurphy's mindless body by choking it to death, and goes over the hill to his own freedom among the wild fields and the flowing rivers—the natural world—of his childhood. McMurphy has set him free, first by returning his hulk to life, then by pointing the way to escape and destroying himself for the sake of the only other truly human figure in the novel.

John A. Barsness, "Ken Kesey: The Hero In Modern Dress," 1969.

At one point, McMurphy characterizes the inmates of the hospital as "victims of a matriarchy." In Kesey's view, modern society is a reflection of womanish values—archetypically responsible, cautious, repressive, deceitful, and solemn. One must look to the spirit of the whore if one would know what is best in women, and what can best bring out what is vital in men. There is no doubt that Kesey labors under a most reactionary myth, involving the mystique of male sexuality, which sees men as intrinsically better than women in terms of the dynamism and strength they can impart to the universe.

Robert Boyers, "Porno Politics," 1968.

[*Cuckoo's Nest's*] very sentimentality, good-guys bad-guys melodrama, occasional obviousness and thinness of texture, I find—like the analogous things in [James Fennimore] Cooper—not incidental flaws, but part of the essential method of its madness. . . .

. . . Everywhere in Kesey, as a matter of fact, the influence of comics and, especially, comic books is clearly perceptible, in the mythology as well as in the style; for like those of many younger writ-ers of the moment, the images and archetypal stories which underlie his fables are not the legends of Greece and Rome, not the fairy tales of Grimm, but the adventures of Captain Marvel and Captain Marvel, Jr., those new-style Supermen who, sometime just after World War II, took over the fantasy of the young.

Leslie Fiedler, The Return of the Vanishing American, *1968.*

Kesey's mode of simplification voices a moral vision rooted in clear-cut opposition between Good and Evil, between natural man and society, between an older mode of existence honoring masculine physical life and a modern day machine culture inimical to it, between the Indian fishing village and the hydroelectric dam. Modern society standardizes men and straitjackets its misfits; it causes the illness which it quarantines. The spiritual residue of the American Old West opposes the machine culture; but the West, as such, is doomed like McMurphy.

> *Terry G. Sherwood, "One Flew Over the Cuckoo's Nest and the Comic Strip," 1971.*

. . . Kesey is systematic in fusing Christian mythology with the American myth of the white man and the noble red man fighting against the encroachment of civilization, represented by women. Though in modern society women are as much subject to the processes of mechanized conformity as men (some say *more*), the inmates of this symbolic hospital are all male, and McMurphy calls them 'victims of a matriarchy.' . . . The novel is comic-book Freud: the man who achieves his manhood (keeping women under him, happy whores in bed) is the free man—he's the buckaroo with the power of laughter.

> *Pauline Kael*, When the Lights Go Down, *1980*

Cuckoo's Nest appears more experimental and unconventional than it actually is. The tone is irreverent and antiestablishment, and the psychotic Indian narrator is original; but for the most part Kesey has made skillful use of well-established techniques and patterns. He draws upon the most familiar of myth patterns—the savior and sacrificial hero, death and rebirth, and the search for the father. He also alludes frequently to popular types from American folk tradition and popular culture. His patterns of imagery are unmistakably explicit and developed in conventional ways, and the structure of the novel is clear and symmetrical. The novel's success results from a skillful application of established literary methods to an apparently icono-clastic theme. The iconoclasm is more apparent than real because the Establishment is largely caricatured and the values asserted are basically those at the heart of Western American Culture.

Stephen L. Tanner, Ken Kesey, 1983.

Big Nurse speaks for the fixed pattern, the unbreak-able routine, the submission of individual will to mechanical, humourless control. McMurphy speaks an older American language of freedom, unhindered movement, self-reliance, anarchic humour and a trust in the more animal instincts.

Tony Tanner, City of Words, 1971

Kesey creates finally in McMurphy a modern unhero or anti-hero who expands himself, through a gradual shift in his concern from himself to those around him, into the role of the traditional hero. It is a strange and preposterous role . . . In the modern world, such a hero, individualistic to the point of disaffiliation but at the same time altruistic to the point of self-sacrifice, is by definition absurd; and all people and actions touched by such heroism are tinted by its absurdity.

Joseph J. Waldmeir, "Two Novelists of the Absurd: Heller and Kesey," 1964.